AEROSPACE BALLOONS

From Montgolfiere To Space

By Edwin J. Kirschner

AERO PUBLISHERS, INC.
329 West Aviation Road, Fallbrook, CA 92028

Library of Congress Cataloging in Publication Data

Kirschner, Edwin J.
    Aerospace balloons.
     Includes index.
     1. Balloons.   2. Expandable space structures.
I. Title.
TL610,K57 1985   629.133'22   85-6001
ISBN 0-8168-0951-8

Printed and Bound in the United States of America.

DEDICATION
This book is especially dedicated to my wife Eleanor, to my children, John, Richard, Caroline and Jacqueline.

ACKNOWLEGDEMENT
I gratefully acknowledge and wish to thank the many people in industry and government for their personal assistance.

PREFACE

Man's earliest thoughts about flying and his earliest attempts at flight took place before the days of science; before man began to measure, to investigate, to experiment and to think things out in orderly fashion. The invention of the balloon in 1783 reveals an example of man's creative genius, his ability to make something new which never existed before.

Dreams of flight were based on examples from our imaginative myths and legends as well as examples of flight observed in nature. By looking at ancient myths, we see man's earliest thoughts and dreams about flight. The best known of the stories of flight is the ancient Greek story of Daedalus and his son Icarus, who built wings fashioned of wax and feathers and used them to escape from prison. During the escape flight, Icarus soared so high that the heat from the sun melted the wax, causing the wings to become detached from his arms and plunging him to his death in the sea. Other legends tell of such imaginary flying schemes as the flying dragon, winged horse, flying carpet, winged sandal, and a chariot drawn across the skies by teams of horses. These devices worked well in story, legend and imagination, but didn't work at all in the real world.

Using examples found in the real world of nature, man first thought of trying to copy the wings of birds and use the energy of the air to fly. Similarly, the flying seeds of some plants were observed to have an aerodynamic, or heavier-than-air, shape which could be lifted by the winds. But the lack of a power source made the search for heavier-than-air flight pointless and there were no aerostatic, or lighter-than-air, examples from nature which had the built-in buoyancy, or lifting power, to carry man aloft.

This principle of buoyancy was discovered by Archimedes, then revived by Roger Bacon in 1250 in his concept of a thin hollow globe filled with inflammable air which could float on air like a vessel floats on water. Following Bacon was Leonardo da Vinci, who experimented with hollow waxen figures filled with warm air. In the century following da Vinci, Evangelista Torricelli produced the first barometer and explored the principle of aerostation which explains how an object can be supported in the air by buoyancy. The Age of Enlightenment brought an end to centuries of occasional inventions and theories, and marked a change to a more rapid pace of advancement in balloon technology. These advancements could not have happened without the courageous, lonely adventures of the great balloon pioneers such as the Montgolfier brothers, de Rozier, d'Arlandes, Charles, Roberts, Lunardi, Yon, Sadler, Garnerin, Spencers, Mallet, Wise, Lowe, Allen, King, Baldwin, Stevens and others who helped chart the beginnings of man's flight into the atmosphere.

By the turn of the Twentieth Century there was an upsurge in higher altitude research and scientific balloon activities. Early balloons were used to study the physical properties of clouds and the atmosphere. Some were equipped with recording instruments, bara-thermo hydrographs and sounding equipment. It was a German professor, Hergesell, who used a small sounding balloon which rose with a perceptibly constant speed and tracked with a chronometer. Hergesell followed the flight of the balloon with a theodlite, which gave him its directional position and hence the speed of the wind. Other scientific balloon experiments were employed to determine the degree of polarization of light and to measure the spectrum of radiation. As basic technical improvements continued, radio transmitters were placed in balloons to signal information on atmospheric pressure, speed, wind direction, temperature and humidity-to-ground receiving stations. The upper atmospheric and aerospace balloons that followed helped carry out fundamental and essential research which has helped to increase our knowledge of such physical sciences as meteorology and astronomy as well as space physics and physiology.

Changes in the use and technology of the balloon have created a need to redefine its accustomed meaning. While the word "balloon" still refers to any object intended to be inflated, particularly by gas; no longer does the balloon have to be hydrostatically lifted by pressure and equilibrium of gases, nor is it restricted to the air surrounding the earth. Today the modern definition of the word "balloon" has come to include devices such as space structures pneumatically erected outside our atmosphere. Also included is the huge space solar antenna which can be folded compactly and transported into space. There, it can be erected pneumatically and placed into operation. Buildings and other facilities can also be carried into space or onto other planetary bodies in a compact unit, to be used for housing, research and development facilities, exploration and for space transportation missions. It is through this modern definition that the balloon takes its natural advancement into the aerospace era with its links to space structure technology, continuing the heritage of ballooning into the future.

TABLE OF CONTENTS

I

AEROSPACE

BALLOON

MILESTONES

Long before Icarus fell from the sky, men dreamed of flying. In that ancient tale of tragedy, Daedalus, intending to flee from the terrible fate of the Labyrinth, decides to escape the island of Minos by fashioning wings and flying away to the mainland. With him he takes Icarus, his son. In some versions of the tale Icarus falls because, enamoured of flight, he forgets his father's warnings about the physical limits of the wings.

What is notable, is that Daedalus—considering flight—designs wings. The implication is that early man imagined flying not as floating in the wind, like the seed of a plant, or spinning through the air like the seeds of some trees, but rather of climbing with beating wings into the sky, and there to soar and glide as a bird. Indeed, in ancient China it is just this desire which led some unknown genius to design the first kite. Yet, in the west it was not principles of aerodynamics that led to our first flying, but rather principles of gravity—it all appears to begin with Archimedes.

Archimedes of Syracuse was a Greek who hailed from the largest city on the island of Sicily when that island was a thriving colony of Cornith; one of the principal city-states of ancient Greece. Archimedes was an inventive genius and the first in the west attributed with conceiving of a vessel light enough to float in air. How he came to consider such an idea is told in the following story:

It seems that the ruler of Syracuse commissioned from a certain goldsmith a crown to be made. However, when finally the goldsmith presented the finished work, the ruler became suspicious that the goldsmith had kept back some of the gold and instead used alloy metals in making the crown. The ruler called for Archimedes, demanding that the inventor discover whether or not the crown was pure gold. To complicate matters the ruler also specified that neither could the crown be destroyed nor could Archimedes declare failure, for if he did either, his life would be forfeit. It seems obvious that such a commission caused the problem of the crown to dominate the inventor's thoughts. Then, one day while taking a bath and mulling over the problem, it came to him. He became so excited that he leaped out of the bath and ran naked through the streets shouting "Eureka," which in Greek means "I found it."

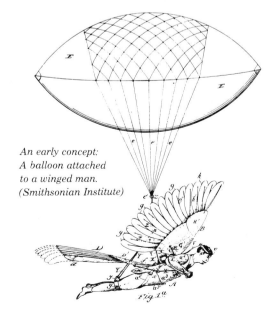

An early concept:
A balloon attached
to a winged man.
(Smithsonian Institute)

What Archimedes had realized was this: that if the crown and an equal volume of pure gold were weighed in air and then again in water, the loss of the weight of the pure gold in water as compared to the crown would be exactly the same—if the crown was also pure. If the weights were not equal, then Archimedes could deduce that the goldsmith had alloyed some other metal with the gold and stolen what he could.

What Archimedes had discovered was the principle of specific gravity; the basic concept for understanding buoyancy. Simply stated, the principle says that a buoyant force exerted by a fluid upon a body immersed in it is equal to the weight of the fluid displaced by the body. What import this had for the goldsmith we cannot know for sure. But it explains plainly why a balloon filled with a gas that is lighter than the surrounding air will float; for such a balloon has a negative displacement.

Yet it took long centuries before the discovery of Archimedes was reconsidered by someone as brilliant as the Syracusan.

When, in 1250, the English wizard-cleric, Roger Bacon, observed that air had an upper surface like a sea upon which suitable forms of flying apparatus could float, he proved that he understood the Archimedean principle. Bacon wrote:

> Such a machine must be a hollow globe of copper, or other suitable metal wrought extremely thin in order to have it as light as possible. This globe must be filled with aethereal (inflammable) air or liquid fire and launched from some elevated point into the atmosphere where it will float like a vessel on water.

Thus, Bacon very simply expressed the basic concept of balloon flight.

In the century following, Bacon's proposition was reaffirmed by Albert of Saxony who also believed the atmosphere could be navigated by flotation. In the century after Albert, Leonardo da Vinci, the universal student, filled notebooks with studies of birds and their wings and designs of flying devices based on wing forms. He also experimented with hollow waxen figures filled with warm air. Da Vinci was very close, with these figures, to the idea of a fabric balloon. Yet, these experiments came near the end of his life, and, as no one had yet proved that air did, in fact, have weight, and, as it was not understood why hot air appeared to rise,

he had little on which to build. Still it was da Vinci who must be credited with beginning the scientific inquiry toward the solution.

During the long period of centuries between Archimedes and da Vinci a certain peculiar idea became established which proposed that fire was a special manifestation of a strange fluid flowing out of some unknown material. The alchemists of Bacon's time named this fluid Flogiston. Scholars trace this idea back to the Greek philosopher, and teacher of Alexander, Aristotle. Aristotle is thought to have lived between 384 and 322 B.C., only a century or so before Archimedes. Aristotle reasoned that all matter was made up of four different kinds: earth, fire, air and water. Today we like to think that what Aristotle meant by earth are those things we call solids; by air what we call gases; and by water what we call liquids. This leaves us wondering what exactly Aristotle meant by fire. The clue seems to lie with the alchemists.

Just as Archimedes was rediscovered during Bacon's time, so was Aristotle, by Bacon and his contemporaries. These medieval inquiries into the nature of matter are generally referred to as alchemists and it is from their writings that we know of Aristotle's ideas. The alchemists such as Bacon were interested in the nature of matter only incidentally. Their primary interests were in learning how to turn base metals into gold and in discovering the "Elixir of Life." While their first pursuits proved vain, yet their incidental pursuits provided a rich ground upon which others might build. It is from the alchemists that we have learned how they, and probably Aristotle, considered "Flogiston."

Because fire and smoke were both observed to rise in the air, fire was correctly considered to be a phenomena rather than a thing. The alchemists reasoned that if fire and smoke were both lighter than air, Flogiston, too, must be lighter than air. This explains why so many early designers and builders of balloons occupied themselves with discussions of filling their balloons with Flogiston. The alchemists, then, are historically important because they posed questions concerning the nature of fire and thus increased interest in the nature of air.

In the next century after da Vinci, four centuries after Bacon, an Italian physicist and mathematician, Evangelista Torricelli (who lived from 1608 to 1647) asked the question, "If air does have weight, how can it be proved?"

He knew from Archimedes that it must. Probably he knew of Leonardo's experiments, so like Leonardo he set up an experiment. What he did was to take a glass tube and seal one end. He then filled the tube with mercury, placing his finger over the open end, so that the mercury could not run out. He turned the tube upside down, placing the open end in a small basin also filled with mercury. Torricelli then removed his finger and allowed the mercury in the tube to run into the basin. The tube did not empty. He observed that the mercury only emptied to a point where the column in the tube stood at a height of about 30 inches above the basin. Understanding the principle of Archimedes, Torricelli correctly reasoned that if the air had weight, then, the air would press down on the surface of the liquid metal in the basin pushing the mercury up into the tube to a height that would produce a pressure in the tube equal to the pressure of the air upon the mercury in the basin. His method was accurate because he had closed the top end of the tube. Thus, the air pressure within the tube was independent of the pressure outside the tube.

Torricelli accurately reasoned that if air had weight the further one went down in air the greater would be the pressure exerted by the air. To make sure of his interpretation he therefore performed his next experiment in reverse.

Torricelli climbed with his experiment to the top of a mountain. There he observed that the pressure of the air measured by his tube of mercury was less than it was at the foot of the mountain. By knowing how far up the mountain he had carried the experiment and by comparing this with the reduction in the air pressure, Torricelli was able to deduce how much air weighed per cubic foot.

With his experiment, Torricelli not only proved that air had weight and exerted pressure like any other gas, but he also provided a means of measuring this weight. His discovery established his as the pivotal figure in the pursuit of the principles of aerostattion, that is, how an object can be supported in air by buoyancy.

The first properly formulated aerostat came from a Jesuit priest named Francesco de Lana-Terzi (1631-1687). Rather than displacing the air in a vessel with Flogiston, de Lana-Terzi reasoned that "no air" is lighter than "some air" and therefore, by removing the air from hollow spherical containers 20 feet in diameter, the containers would float upward. His mathematics gave evidence that this "vacuum balloon" could have a metal skin lighter than the weight of the air removed from its interior. Unfortunately, the technology was not available to make the sphere the priest designed!

Early in the Eighteenth Century, possibly the year 1709, another inventor, Bartolomeu Lourenco de Gusmao, exhibited at the court at Lisbon a ball propelled to the roof by combustion. Before his death in 1724, he had designed a hot air balloon, an airship filled with gas and an airplane. None of these were built, but the existence of his designs prove the thrust of the new age.

Coming after Gusmao, a Dominican friar named Joseph Galien theorized that air must vary in density from sea level to high

Francis Lana, designer of vacuum balloon—1670.
(Smithsonian Institute)

altitudes. He believed that one might be able to navigate the denser regions of the earth's atmosphere by capturing a large mass of lighter air from higher altitudes and putting it in an airship. Galien did not have a puny imagination; in 1755, he suggested an airship containing approximately 100 million cubic feet of upper atmosphere which thus provides for a total lifting force at sea level of about 7,500 million pounds!

In England, a contemporary of Galien's, a chemist, Henry Cavendish (1731-1810) while mixing iron, tin and zinc shavings with oil in vitriol during an experiment, discovered a gas he named "inflammable air." This discovery was not taken to be of great import by Cavendish himself, yet another English chemist named Joseph Black, who knew of Cavendish's find, was prompted in 1768 to propose a thin, light bladder filled with "inflammable air." Sometime later, the French chemist Lavoisier, renamed the gas "hydrogene." In 1782, a year before the first public demonstration of the hot air balloon, an Italian physicist, Tiberius Cavalio, then living in England, succeeded in getting soap bubbles to float upward after inflating them with "hydrogen" gas.

The Age of Enlightenment brought a marked change in the pace at which men examined the world around them. It no longer required a century for the invention and theory of one man to prompt another as it had between Bacon and da Vinci or da Vinci and Torricelli. Sixteen years after Cavendish made his discovery; one year after Cavalio's demonstration, two brothers in France were planning to make smoke clouds that would fly when placed in a lightweight bag. Joseph and Jacques Montgolfier made many experiments and finally, in 1782, achieved success.

Their original test balloon was made of a silky linen opened at the bottom. When flaming paper was held near the opening, the oblong paper bag, called a "balon," slowly filled out with hot air and floated upward.

One hundred and twenty years before powered flight at Kitty Hawk, the first flight in history took place on November 21, 1783 . . .the invention of the Montgolfier brothers from Annonary, France, who developed it into its practical form. The "Montgolfiere," or hot-air balloon, as this type became known, was launched by first suspending it limp between the two masts shown in the sketch. A fire was then lit beneath the hole in the platform to inflate the balloon by using the heated air. (Author)

Joseph Montgolfier

One of the Montgolfier brothers who is credited with the invention of the balloon. (Smithsonian Institute)

Thus, the Montgolfier brothers anticipated the Wright brothers by over 120 years!

The size of their initial test balloons ranged from 40 cubic feet capacity to 650 cubic feet. These balloons ascended from 90 to 600 feet in the air.

Having tested progressively larger balloons in relative privacy, the Montgolfiers finally made ready to test one publicly. On June 5, 1783, the brothers made ready a linen balloon, its sections joined together with buttons. Inflated over a fire fed with small bundles of chopped straw, the 23,430-cubic-foot balloon, 105 feet in circumference, ascended from the marketplace at Annony, France to an altitude of 6,000 feet. People promptly named it a "Montgolfiere."

Three months later, on September 19, 1783, a larger Montgolfiere, made of linen and paper, was flown from Versailles by Joseph who controlled guide ropes from the ground below. As aviation's first airborne passengers, the 41-foot-diameter, 86-foot-high balloon carried, in a wicker basket slung underneath, a sheep, a duck and a rooster. All were returned safely to earth. These first Montgolfiere balloons, while providing the possibility of flight, also proved to be of limited endurance for, as the air in the bag cooled, the balloon was forced to descend.

Those experimenting with hydrogen had no such problems. On August 27, 1783, a month and a few weeks after the first public flight of the Montgolfiere's, Professor Jaques Alexandre C. Charles launched a balloon inflated with hydrogen gas from the heart of Paris during a drizzling rain. Charles, who was a physicist, shared his achievement with his associates, the Robert brothers, Charles and M.N. Robert. Their balloon, a spherical bag of lute-string silk, measured 13 feet in diameter and was impregnated with an elastic gum to render it gas tight. The hydrogene was produced by placing iron filings in a compartment and dripping diluted sulfuric acid from above. The flight was a free flight with the balloon ascending from the Place des Victories to a height of approximately 3,000 feet and descending some 15 miles away.

Unlike the open-necked Montgolfieres, the first "Charliere" balloon was closed by a valve to contain the gas. When it landed well outside the city, terrified peasants attacked the balloon with pitchforks, tied it to a horse's tail and dragged it across the countryside. In response to this incident Louis XVI's government was prompted to issue a proclamation that balloons were harmless!

The stage having been set, the finale followed quickly. On Octrober 15, 1783, a minor member of the second estate, one Jean F.P. de Rozier made several tethered ascents during the day rising up to 80 feet during one brief 5-minute flight. For this flight de Rozier used an oval Montgolfiere of 60,000-cubic-foot capacity. He stood in a circular gallery while a fire in a central grate provided the lift. In this same gaily colored aerostat, on November 21, 1783, de Rozier and his friend Marquis Francois Laurent d' Arlandes flew free from the Bois de Boulogne to a height of 500 feet, traveling, in 20 minutes, to a landing some 5 miles away.

Among the onlookers the day of the de Rozier flight were the King and Queen of France and the U.S. envoy Benjamin Franklin.

Certainly alive to the sense of a new age dawning Franklin wrote of the flight:

> The invention of the balloon appears to be a discovering of great important and what may possibly give a new turn to human affairs. Convincing soverigns of the folly of wars may perhaps be one effect of it, since it will be impractical for the most potent of them to guard his dominions. Five thousand balloons capable of raising two men each, could not cost more than five ships of the line; and where is the prince who could afford so to cover his country with troops for its defense that 10,000 men descending from the clouds might not in many places do an infinite mischief before a force could be brought to repel them.

Of course, Franklin's hope could not come to pass in an age so ripe for revolution, yet, even though there were balloonists serving in Napoleon's Grand Armee, there were also an increasing number of individuals who set

Hydrogen-filled Charles' passenger balloon, December 1, 1783. (Smithsonian Institute)

11

their allegiance to science before other things and for whom the balloon appeared a tool of enlightenment.

With the earliest flights an era of scientific research and practical ballooning blossomed that was to yield considerable knowledge. Information was sought on air currents, temperature, and pressure variations, and wind velocity in the atmosphere. One Dr. Jefferies, an American physician, carried out barometric, thermometric, and hygrometric observations by balloons over London during the early 1780's! (On one of his flights in 1784, Dr. Jefferies systematically obtained samplings of air at differing altitudes; perhaps the first such sampling of its kind.)

Another early balloonist-scientist was French physicist and chemist Joseph Gay-Lussac. In several flights he recorded reaching altitudes up to 23,000 feet. This was the year 1804. It was Gay-Lussac's experiences at altitude, the quickening of the pulse, gasping for air and finally unconciousness revealed the danger of high altitude ascents. For almost a half-century following Gay-Lussac there was a distinct lessening of activity due to the perplexing nature of this phenomenon. Finally, in 1859, the British

Early aeronauts, Guy-Lussac and brother, ascent of August 23, 1804. *(Smithsonian Institute)*

Association for the Advancement of Science (BAAS) initiated a program for making observations at the higher altitudes of the atmosphere using the balloon. Once more, men began to consider the balloon as an instrument of science.

Few would dispute the importance for the science of the first BAAS flights made by the two Englishmen, Henry Coxwell, an aeronaut, and James Glaisher, a respected scientist. It was Coxwell who constructed in 1862 a 90,000-cubic-foot balloon for meteorological and scientific investigations. Coxwell and Glaisher made their first flight in July at Wolveringhamton, England, which became the first of 27 succeeding ascents. The last of these took place on May 26, 1866.

In this series of flights the two were out to establish, among other things, a world record for high altitude. This nearly cost them their lives. On September 5, 1862, Coxwell and Glaisher took off early in the morning, without oxygen equipment, in an open gondola. In forty minutes they were at 21,000 feet and still rising. Both became drowsy in the thin air. Glaisher lost conciousness as Coxwell struggled to valve out the hydrogen but the valve was frozen or stuck. Hands frozen, he frantically stuck the rope in his mouth and pulled. The valve opened, the hydrogen flowed out and the

Robert Brothers' dirigible, 1784. *(Smithsonian Institute)*

Channel balloon crossing by Blanchard and Jefferies, 1784. *(Smithsonian Institute)*

casions a camera was carried aloft as well as an electrometer, to detect and measure electrical charges and potential differences. Few pioneering scientists have been as thorough as James Glaisher. And even as Glaisher systematically tested the scientific potentials of the balloon, a contemporary of his systematically speculated on the kind of world suggested by inventions such as the balloon.

Jules Verne's balloons, dirigibles, and imaginative journeys, even into outer space, certainly began to prepare society for the technological world that was to come. Enthralled by inventions generally, the Frenchman was absolutely fascinated by the balloon. His inspiration came, in part, from several unique events. One of these was the first balloon crossing of the Alps by a French aeronaut called "Arban," who succeeded in navigating from Marseille, to land in Turin. Another might have been the Austrian Army's bombardment of the city of Venice using 100 pilotless, hot air balloons, each equipped with a time bomb. (While most of these carried away from the city, and some even drifted back into the Austrian lines, the event remained singular and was widely publicized.)

balloon descended. On the ground, they checked the recording instrument and found that they had reached a record altitude of 37,000 feet.

Each of the many flights by Coxwell and Glaisher was made for a specific scientific purpose. Equipment carried aloft helped to determine the air temperature and measure the atmospheric moisture at different elevations; temperature was taken at dew point using a hygrometer; they used dry and wet thermometers for comparative temperatures; made comparable measurements using both an aneroid barometer and mercurial type; the two investigated the electrical state of air; examined the oxygenic conditions of the atmosphere; observed magnetic vibrations; took air samplings at different altitudes; decided the direction and velocity of the atmospheric currents at different altitudes; determined the types and heights of clouds, their density and thickness; and they also attempted to account for sounds at different altitudes. On several oc-

In the presence of President George Washington, one of the first air voyages in America was made by Jean Pierre Blanchard in a balloon from Philadelphia, January 9, 1793. Blanchard carried the first air letter, a passport of introduction, from President Washington. *(Smithsonian Institute)*

These widely publicized balloon exploits combined with the publication of Edgar Allen Poe's story, "Balloon Hoax," which described a three-day balloon flight across the Atlantic, sparked Verne. He became so interested in balloons and ballooning that he personally gathered and read every available technical source in addition to seeking out and interviewing many notable scientists and balloonists. This done, he wrote a story entitled "A Balloon Journey." This story foreshadowed by many years any other novels about flight and helped to establish Verne as the father of science fiction.

Enthused with the mission of making ballooning popular, one of Verne's acquaintances, Felix Tournchon, who was known to all Paris as "Nadar," set out in 1861, to build the world's largest, most luxurious, passenger balloon. Nadar had made his name as a writer, pioneer photographer and balloonist. (In 1858, it was he who took history's first aerial photo, from a balloon above Paris.) His abilities as a promoter resulted in the "Geant" (Giant), a 210,000-cubic-foot balloon made from thousands of yards of Lyons' silk. The passenger car was big enough to hold a dozen people and was equipped with double-decker bunks, a kitchen and a darkroom. The Geant was in the final stages of construction when Verne released a new book entitled "Five Weeks In A Balloon," which promptly captured the imagination of an avid public.

On the fourth of October, 1863, the Geant lifted to its first ascent. From the Champs de Mars, the traditional balloon launching site in Paris, Nadar, his wife, the aeronauts Jules and Louis Godard, and a few intrepit others, sailed comfortably to a landing 25 miles away at Meux. The principal mission of those ensconced in the comforts of the two-story, wicker-work car was to sit down to a meal of "ham, fowl and dessert." After such an auspicious beginning everything seemed perfect for the promise of the second flight. On October 18, just a few weeks after her inaugural voyage, the Geant set out on what was to prove a 400-mile trial of wind and storm. Nadar, fearfully mistaking a cloud bank for the surface of the North Sea, fought the balloon down in a high wind near Hanover, Germany. Demolishing everything in its path, the Geant finally came to rest. Miraculous-

Nadar's giant balloon at Paris in 1853. This sumptuous two-story gondola was made of wicker. Le Geant was the largest balloon made up to that time. (Library of Congress)

ly, there were no casualties. Nadar continued to exhibit the craft on tours throughout the continent, but never flew it again.

Notwithstanding the efforts and imagination of all these, the problem of altitude remained to be solved.

When in 1903 the brilliant Russian, Konstanin E. Tsiolkovsky published his scientific paper entitled, "The Exploration of Cosmic Space by Means of Reaction Motors," he plainly heralded the opening of the Aerospace Era. Tsiolkovsky's work examined the use of fuels and rockets for space flight. His paper was to influence two important pioneers; Robert H. Goddard of the U.S.A., and Herman J. Oberth, a Hungarian who later became a German citizen. By 1919 Goddard had published a book on rocketry and, in 1926, it was he who fired the first liquid-fueled rocket. Oberth, meanwhile, authored papers examining how rockets could be made to escape earth's gravitational pull. It was not until the mid-1950's when the inflatable space balloon and the rocket were combined to prepare for the exploration of space beyond the earth's atmosphere.

Working independently, lit by the spark

Franco-Prussian War, 1870–1871—Manufacture of balloons within railroad stations (the works of Godard in the Orleans Station, Paris). During the seige of Paris, Felix Nadar organized a mail and passenger emergency service by balloon.
(Smithsonian Institute)

of Tsiolkovsky's imagination, Oberth and Goddard were the first to wrestle with the technical issues of rocketry and high-altitude research. It was their efforts that succeeded in awakening the scientific community's interest in space and space travel.

But, it was balloons, not rockets, which first took men to the very limits of the atmosphere where the life-sustaining envelope of earth verges on the vast emptiness of space. And just as in Guy-Lussac's time, it was the problem of pressure, not the problem of gravity, which faced the aeronauts of the early decades of this Twentieth Century.

With two separate ascents in 1931 and 1932, the Swiss physicist Auguste Piccard took the lead in the climb upward. In his first flight Piccard and an assistant lifted off from Augsberg, Germany inside an enclosed, pressurized, spherical gondola made of aluminum. Suspended from a rubberized, hydrogen filled balloon, they attained the record altitude of 51,961 feet. On the second flight, again with an assistant, the old record was broken, the gondola reaching an altitude of 53,139 feet.

Not only had Piccard reached into the stratosphere ... where no man had gone before ... but while there, was able to glean new information on the nature of gamma rays and cosmic rays as they exit earth's atmosphere. Compounding his success was the unique design and operation of his balloon; this became his major contribution to the scientific efforts of his time.

In the next year, on November 20, 1933, Navy Lieutenant Commander T.G.W. Settle and Marine Major C.L. Fordney climbed into the gondola of their 105-foot balloon named, "The Century of Progress." This giant lifted to a new record height of 61,237 feet. Like Piccard, they used a sealed cabin and life-support system making them pioneers in the development of those systems now being used in the manned space program. The flight of the "Century" was notable also for one particular response engendered at the time. Congratulations and challenge came from the USSR's then foreign minister, M. Litvinoff, who declared, "May both our countries continue to contest the heights in every sphere of science and technique." Litvinoff's pronouncement was made all the more singular and moving by events occurring only 50 days earlier. Then, three Russian aeronauts; Prokofier, Gudonov and Birnbaum, also using a sealed, high-altitude cabin, had flown their balloon to an un-

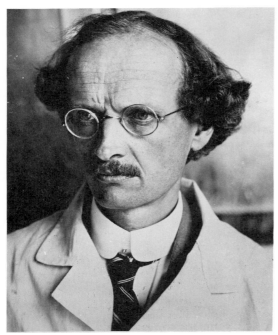

The famous Belgian professor, August Piccard, before his contemplated flight into the "stratosphere." He used a specially constructed globe-like balloon with a cabin full of scientific instruments to ascend to a height never before attained, over 50,000 feet.   *(Underwood Photo)*

The balloon containing Professor Piccard and his assistant, Charles Kipfer, just after leaving the ground on their trip into the stratosphere, to set a record of more than ten miles.
(Underwood Photo)

official record altitude. Unfortunately, something then went wrong with their balloon causing the gondola to plunge to earth, killing all three.

This tragedy and the American success were to become but the first episode in a truly great race; a race, presently, still on course.

The renaissance of aerospace scientific development came about at the end of the Second World War with the advent of new materials in balloon design and construction. Dr. Otto C. Winzen, an American, developed a light, resistant plastic material he called polyethylene. It was polyethylene which spearheaded the economical production of large balloons, and was a required preliminary to the U.S. space program.

It was O.C. Winzen, enthused by the ideas of Piccard, who convinced the U.S. Navy and General Mills, Inc., to launch Project Helios in 1946. The Helios aerostat was made up of 80 plastic-film balloons of 250,000-cubic-foot capacity. And it was Winzen and his new material that encouraged the Office of Naval Research to initiate the Skyhook balloon program in 1947. The early flights soared into the atmosphere to study cosmic rays and high-energy nuclear particles from outer space. The program continues today.

A glimpse of scientific packaging to come. Conducting final inspection of an instrumentation capsule before sealing prior to balloon launch at Ames Research Center. (NASA Photo)

II

DEVELOPMENTS

OF THE '50s

By 1950, polyethylene plastic had clearly demonstrated its superiority to natural or synthetic rubber in high altitude operations. Scientists were elated. With ninty-nine percent of the earth's atmospheric mass lying below 100,000 feet, scientific experiments at or above this level could avoid most of the atmospheric "noise" encountered by lower altitude platforms.

In September of that year, a successful animal-borne balloon flight had taken eight white mice to an altitude of 97,000 feet in a series of tests measuring effects of exposure to cosmic radiation. By 1950, most of the knowledge gained on primary cosmic radiation had been gathered by balloon platforms floating near the top of the atmosphere. But questions about cosmic radiation were not the only questions being answered in those early days when the big transparent balloons were new. Balloons were being sent aloft to obtain vital information concerning the concentration of ozone, carbon dioxide, carbon 14 and nitrous oxide at altitudes up to and exceeding 100,000 feet. Experiments obtaining data on the isotope ratios of oxygen and nitrogen; the presence of radioactive dust raised by nuclear blasts;and long-range weather reconnaissance were also in process.

In 1952, while seeking ways to put a radar-reflective balloon into the eye of a hurricane the U.S. Navy pioneered the air-launching of balloons.

In that same year, a Coast Guard icebreaker loaded with balloons and rockets, set out to conduct stratospheric experiments in the polar regions. The expedition conducted a series of high-altitude studies of cosmic rays in the vicinity of the geo-magnetic pole, north of Greenland. The purpose was to measure the charge of energy in cosmic rays and the interaction of cosmic radiation with the earth's atmosphere at heights between 20 and 70 miles above the earth's surface. Professor James A. Van Allen, after whom the Van Allen belt is named, was a member of the team in charge of the polar rocket project. The arctic launch of a rocket from a balloon platform was first accomplished by professor Van Allen's team on this occasion. This device, popularly called a "Rockoon," was a very simple combination of technologies. To the balloon was attached a gondola which carried the rocket equipment and a variety of compact stratospheric experiments. The balloon rose to approximately 70,000 feet, whereupon a pressure switch inside the gondola closed. This set off the ignition of the "Deacon" rocket which then shot upward. After only seconds the fuel was gone but momentum carried the rocket to an altitude of 300,000 feet. As the rocket plummeted back into the atmosphere, instruments located in the nose cone recorded data on cosmic rays, pressures, heat and other conditions; the data being telemetered to the ship full of excited scientists below.

Balloon rocket launches were in full swing during the mid-1950s, being sent aloft from shipboard, polar sites and also from sites in New Mexico. In one of these launches a captured German V-2 combined with a "Corporal" rocket rose to an altitude of 250 miles. Balloon launch, combined with a single- or multi-stage rocket proved economical means for exploring higher altitudes. The "Rockoons" and BATO (Balloon Assisted Take-Off) could at this time consistently achieve heights of around 300,000 feet.

A series of live bailouts from a balloon gondola at altitudes ranging up to 100,000 feet began in the spring of 1953. Known as the High-Dive Project, this was part of the Defense Department's study of high altitude escape procedures. High-Dive and Project Man-High were closely related efforts, to assess various types of escape equipment and the balloon launching of special re-entry vehicles.

Two years later, the first manned polyethylene balloon flight was attempted by U.S. Navy Commanders Ross and Lewis on November 8, 1956. A defective valve caused the two to abort the flight at 75,787 feet. Eight months after this Navy disappointment, on June 2, 1957, Air Force Captain J.W. Kittenger, using an aerodynamically shaped craft, reached 96,128 feet after rising for one hour and 15 minutes. The month following this, on August 19, 1957, Air Force Major Simons succeeded in a record flight which reached nearly 102,000 feet and lasted 32 hours, 16 of which were spent above 90,000 feet. Major Simons, both a physician and a physicist, made the lighter than air flight in an eight-foot metal capsule attached to a 280-foot-high, polyethylene

Captain Joseph Kittinger seated in USAF Manhigh I capsule which he flew in June 1952 to 96,000 feet for seven hours. Manhigh II was flown by Major D. G. Simons on August 19, 1957 to 101,500 feet for 32 hours. Manhigh III was flown by Lt. Clifton McClure on October 8, 1958 to 100,000 feet for twelve hours.   *(Winzen International)*

balloon filled with helium. The intent of this Man-High II flight was to investigate the near space environment and its effect on human beings.

A benchmark achievement in the use of balloon-rocket technology occurred in 1957 with the Air Force Project Farside. Aiming at unprecedented altitudes, in fact, intending to place research instruments into outer space, the goal of the project was to climb 4,000 miles above the earth!

Using five-stage rockets slung beneath Navy Skyhook balloons the early tests conducted at Eniwetok Atoll were only partially successful. However, one of the project's rockets did rise some 3,000 miles high, reaching outer space.

Another program stemming from the Navy Skyhook efforts was the Strato-Lab Program. This was a continuing series of manned-balloon flights into both the upper and lower atmosphere. By 1956 this program had gleaned valuable geophysical observations; acquired much aero-medical research data on its flight crews and carried out many astrophysical investigations. Succeeding flights studied our sun, planets and the stars beyond our system.

(a) Breakthroughs in Design

The '50s brought several important breakthroughs in the design of balloons. One was the Natural Shape Balloon. This type of balloon, by virtue of the contour of the envelope being determined by the gas "head," induced all stresses to be carried in the vertical line. The other, the super-pressure balloon, was "discovered" in 1956 when the Air Force Cambridge Laboratories (AFCRL) launched a series of small, mylar balloons on a test flight which tracked from Denver to the east coast.

The super-pressure, in contrast to the huge zero-pressure types, did not use acres of polyethylene which expanded as the balloon rose. This type of balloon is a non-extensible, inelastic aerostat, well sealed to prevent helium gas release. Float duration is only limited by the effects of solar radiation on the material of the balloon. It converts the excess gas, with which it is pumped, from free lift at launch, to overpressure at float level. Variations in the radiation at altitude cause pressure changes within the balloon, however, no changes in volume. With a tight balloon the amount of overpressure is equal to the free lift plus superheat.

On September 25, 1957, the sharpest photographs yet taken of the sun were secured by means of a telescope launched on a giant, unmanned Skyhook balloon as a part of the office of Naval Research's project Stratoscope. The Stratoscope balloon was equipped with a special light-sensitive pointing mechanism, and a powerful, specially-designed, twelve-inch astronomical telescope coupled to a 35mm motion picture camera. Stratoscope was the latest effort in the use of Skyhook balloons in exploration of the upper atmosphere initiated by the Office of Naval Research 1946.

(U.S. Navy Photo)

Large super-pressure balloons were launched using a tow balloon to support the ballast. The ballast equals the free lift and is dispensed after reaching altitude. The super-pressure balloon manifests positive differential pressure, stability and long, unballasted flight. Large balloons, while occasionally used for attaining extreme altitudes, are principally used for carrying heavier loads.

(b) Super-pressure Balloons

From the late 1950s, the U.S. Air Force designed and tested super-pressure, spherical balloons mostly in the class of 120-foot diameter and 300-pound payload. But with the development of polyester films and bitape sealing, the super-pressure came into its own as a weather type. Extremely efficient as wind tracers in the field of meteorology, the wide use of super-pressures followed the development of durable lightweight electronics and the early evolution of command telemetry.

Long-duration balloons continue to be developed today; for example, tracking has been improved by use of on-board computers such as used in the Omega system. Control range has been improved through new command systems with greater-than-radio-horizon reach; balloon design and launch

Superpressure spherical balloon, while somewhat larger, is similar in design and contruction to the twelve balloons used in the Forbes Magazine's *Atlantic Project.*
(National Center for Atmospheric Research/NSF)

Small superpressure balloons are used in a global meteorological experiments. Balloons of this type have remained aloft for as much as 744 days.
(National Center for Atmospheric Research/NSF)

technique are also areas yielding to refinement.

Balloon flights with 4,000 to 5,000 pounds of payload have been quite common; lifted by balloons in excess of 20 million cubic feet. One notable example was the June 1975 flight of a 52-million-cubic-foot balloon carrying a 3,100-pound payload. (Payloads in excess of 10,000 pounds have since been flown with special balloon systems.)

(c) Zero-pressure Balloons

Not only were balloons made better during the decade of the '50s, but bigger, too.

Several enormous balloons of the zero-pressure type were launched in 1958 and '59. In November 1958, the first military plastic balloon, 3.75 million cubic feet of 2 mil. polyethylene, was launched as part of a high-mach parachute test. Then in 1959, a six-million-cubic-foot monster carried a 94-pound payload to an altitude of 149,000 feet; a significant accomplishment in those days.

Extreme altitudes, above 170,000 feet are achieved only by minimizing balloon weights and designing for maximum distribution of stress. Zero-pressure balloons

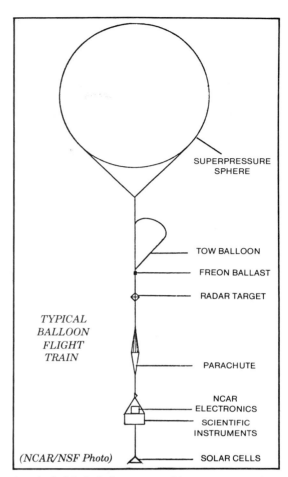

SUPERPRESSURE SPHERE

TOW BALLOON

FREON BALLAST

RADAR TARGET

TYPICAL BALLOON FLIGHT TRAIN

PARACHUTE

NCAR ELECTRONICS

SCIENTIFIC INSTRUMENTS

SOLAR CELLS

(NCAR/NSF Photo)

A typical global circling, recoverable superpressure (non-extensible closed) balloon carrying a scientific payload at 80,000 feet. Completed on March 1, 1973, it made two orbits of the globe in 36 days. *(NCAR/NSF Drawing)*

answer these requirements better than any other type and have, since the '50s become associated with high altitude achievements.

High-altitude balloons have played an important role in magnetosphere research, exploring the solar wind, magnetospheric interactions, plasma convection, the origin of radiation belts and interaction of diverse plasma wave particles. It was a balloon-borne flight that first detected the existence of solar cosmic rays in 1958.

High-altitude, tethered aerostats have applications in defense, telecommunications and broadcast functions. A single airborne communications payload, suspended from an aerostat at an altitude of 10,000 feet, provides coverage over distances of 250 miles and serves a ground area greater than 50,000 square miles. At 15,000 feet, the operating payload range increases to 300 miles and the ground area coverage exceeds 70,000 square miles.

Wallops Flight Center disclosed

Superpressure balloon. *(National Center for Atmospheric Research/National Science Foundation)*

NASA's high-altitude, remotely-controlled aerostats, powered by microwave energy beamed from earth, were used as a platform operating up to 70,000 feet for telecommunications, earth surveillance, in-situ measurements and remote sensing.

Other experiments performed by balloons during the '50s extended into such diverse areas as laser experiments, examination of air pollutants and photographic and spectrographic studies of the Sun and Venus. These last mentioned performed with a manually-operated, servo-stabilized telescope.

Due in major part to the success of aerospace balloons, the sheer volume of experimentation in the United States became partitioned and institutionalized under the auspices of several government agencies. NASA, or the National Aeronautics and Space Administration, is probably the most well known of these.

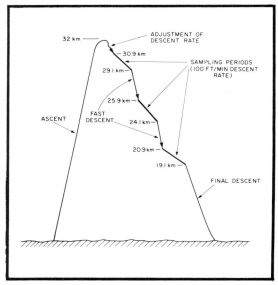

U.S. Air Air Force (ESD/PAM) Photo

MANNED FLIGHTS

	Payload	Maximum Altitude	Duration
U.S.N. STRATOLAB II	3300 lbs.	86,000 ft.	10 hrs.
U.S.N. STRATOLAB III	4000 lbs.	82,000 ft.	34 hrs. 30 min.
U.S.N. STRATOLAB IV	4100 lbs.	81,000 ft.	28 hrs. 15 min.
U.S.N. STRATOLAB V	2280 lbs.	113,740 ft.	9 hrs.
U.S.A.F. MANHIGH I	1350 lbs.	96,000 ft.	7 hrs.
U.S.A.F. MANHIGH II	1750 lbs.	101,500 ft.	32 hrs. 10 min.
U.S.A.F. MANHIGH III	1750 lbs.	100,000 ft.	12 hrs.

List of major manned balloon operations conducted by Winzen Research Inc. in the 1950's for the U.S. Navy and the U.S. Air Force as forerunners of manned space flight.   *(Winzen Research Photo)*

III

ADVANCES

OF THE '60s & '70s

(a) NASA & Other Government Agencies

NASA maintains a significant scientific balloon program which plays an important role in the agency's scientific investigations. Subjects under study include upper-atmospheric research, high-energy astrophysics, stratosphric composition, meteorology, aeronomy and astronomy. The program is supervised from the Wallops Flight Center in Virginia.

The Center manages, monitors, schedules and provides technical analysis for NASA's balloon activities, as well as assistance to the Office of Naval Research and the National Science Foundation.

More than half of the balloons sent up by NASA begin their journey at the National Scientific Balloon Facility (NSBF), located in Palestine, Texas. The balloons which study the skies of the southern hemisphere have been launched in Australia. NASA balloon flight systems and operational support are provided through a number of sources: NSBF at Palestine; the National Research Council of Canada at Ottowa, and the Air Force Geophysics Laboratory in Massachusetts.

While most of Wallop's missions are flown and supported by the NSBF, some of the balloons are launched from other locations situated at Malden, Missouri; Pierre, South Dakota; Holloman Air Force Base in New Mexico; Alice Springs, Australia; Yorkton, Canada; New Zealand; Argentina and Brazil.

In a recent two-year period, Wallops Flight Center supported about 120 balloon missions, representing 19 universities and ten scientific groups. The Center provided ground instrumentation, technical support and flight hardware support to the experimenters through the NASA balloon program.

In the year 1960, two years after NASA formally came into being, the National Center for Atmospheric Research (NCAR) was created to provide a focus on atmospheric research of both national and global scale. NCAR was sponsored directly by the National Science Foundation and operated by the nonprofit University Corporation for Atmospheric Research which is comprised of more than 40 universities with graduate programs in the atmospheric sciences. Just recently, however, NASA has taken over the responsibility of budgeting and operating the NCAR programs.

While NCAR's headquarters are located in Boulder, Colorado, its balloon launch facilities are located in Palestine, Texas, along with those of the National Scientific Balloon Facility. The NSBF was established in 1961, under NCAR auspices, and both facilities were situated on the same former Army Air Corps base. The NSBF director and his staff have undertaken the challenge of the scientific community's demands for heavier payloads, higher altitudes, and longer periods, with a high success rate.

Three NSBF divisions provide the technical services necessary for each balloon flight: Meteorology provides information and forecasts for all meteorological parameters concerned with balloon flight; Flight Electronics prepares the data retrieval system and electronics for the gondola and balloon control; Flight Operations furnishes interface team to the scientific team from bal-

The National Scientific Balloon Facility (NSBF) in Palestine, Texas. The site consists of an asphalt launch area arranged with six arms which radiate through a 180-degree arc to permit launch with the wind blowing in any direction. An operations/laboratory building, machine shop and various specially built launch and radar vehicles. *(NCAR Photo)*

Mammoth balloon launch in July 1966. *(NCAR Photo)*

Double-balloon launch from NCAR Scientific Balloon Flight Station, Palestine, Texas, November 13, 1964. The tandem balloon system shown here, shortly before its early morning launch from Palestine, was sent aloft equipped with cameras to test the feasibility of photographing the stresses on a balloon as it ascends through the tropopause. The flight was part of NCAR's efforts to improve the performance and reliability of balloons as unmanned vehicles for scientific research. *(NASA Photo)*

loon to gondola, and launch, tracking and recovery services.

In a typical flight, the scientists usually bring their instruments to one of the operating sites, and spend between a week and a month in final instrument preparation and checkout. The balloon crew is then responsible for attaching the scientific package to the balloon, as well as the launch, tracking and recovery of the instrument. Often there is a wait of several days after the instrument is ready before suitable launch weather arrives with surface winds of less than 17 feet per second and minimal cloud cover.

Once launched, the balloon ascends to the float altitude in two to four hours and will then float at a constant altitude for several hours to two or three days. Throughout the flight, the scientific package hangs from a parachute which in turn is attached to the base of the balloon. On a radio command, the parachute is separated from the balloon and the package falls to the ground under the open chute, while the balloon is destroyed and falls separately. The instruments are recovered and often flown again.

Normally, each balloon carries one scientific instrument set and the control package provided by the balloon crew for tracking and radio command. Scientific data can be recorded on board or telemetered during the flight, using either a downlink provided by the balloon crew or one provided by the scientists themselves. Small, simple experiments are sometimes flown as "hitchhikers" on a balloon principally devoted to another, larger instrument. However, flights with more than one instrument package are rare.

In 1961, through an international agency, a program was set up called GARP (Global Atmospheric Research Program). This program concentrates on the problems of long-range forecasting, atmospheric fluctuations that control changes in weather and on designing a suitable observational system for systematizing global investigations. In a plan for the '70s GARP outlined requirements for primary world measurements of wind, temperature, pressure and humidity.

NASA's Ames Research Center reported in 1977 on large orbiting solar reflectors and described the SOLARES design as the one providing large amounts of solar energy reflected to Earth collector sites for conversion to electrical power. The design of the SOLARES spacecraft showed a rigid toroi-

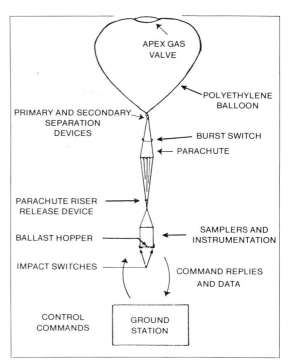

Typical Sampling System Flight Configuration   *(NCAR)*

dal structure which was very similar to an earlier inflatable reflector introduced by NASA Aerospace Technologist John E. Canady, Jr., at the Langley Reserach Center. The inflatable solar reflector employed gas to inflate the torus and expand the structure. The skin of the torus with the other structural elements were impregnated with a gel of polyurethane which had a volatile solvent plasticizer that evaporated soon after the structure expanded and was exposed to the hard vacuum of space.

This structural design was no longer dependent upon pressurized gas for maintaining its shape and rigidity. The Langley Center has continued to examine and evaluate solar energy systems within its general systems studies of orbiting reflectors. It was concluded in the late 1970's that it was possible to package an inflatable 1-kilometer reflector spacecraft in a single space shuttle.

ASH CAN ... a descriptive title given to this balloon system's payload and used by the Atomic Energy Commission (now the Department of Energy) to monitor radioactivity in the environment. Launches began in 1956, collecting stratospheric particulate air samples from various locations. In 1966 the project expanded concurrently with air-launched, air-recoverable rockets which placed payloads at higher altitudes than with a balloon alone. The DOD's Advanced Research Project Agency cosponsored with

SEAT STABILIZATION
DROGUE CHUTE

BALLOON IN PARACHUTE
SHAPE CONFIGURATION

INITIAL CONVERSION
FROM PARACHUTE TO
BALLOON SHAPE

Page 26 and 27:

Pilot Aerial Survival System (PASS), an ejection seat escape technique developed in 1967 was a change from the manual pilot bailout from his aircraft over hostile territory. PASS increases the pilot's survivability, by allowing the pilot to eject and remain airborne for an extended period of time before a mid-air retrieval is made by a rescue aircraft. The primary components of PASS are a combination parachute/balloon which is packed and deployed in the same manner as a conventional ejection-seat parachute. The difference was integrating the bouyancy of a recovery hotair aerostat into the parachute system. (Raven Industries)

AEC the further development of a detection system for monitoring nuclear activities. The balloon selected was made of Stratofilm polyethylene material produced by Winzen Research and the first one was delivered to the USAF Air Weather Service in 1964.

Ash Can, using a 250,000-cubic-foot sized balloon, had an 80,000-foot float altitude; with a 10.6-million-cubic-foot balloon, an altitude of 135,000 feet could be reached. Its payload weighed between 370 and 500 pounds depending on the air sampler used. The sampler, designed by Litton Industries, moved large volumes of air at high altitudes through filter paper which collected the particulate debris for laboratory analysis.

Likewise, the USAF Aerospace Rescue and Recovery Service supported the AEC's upper atmospheric nuclear debris investigations which yielded a separately new application for mid-air rescue of parachuting airmen. This tandem parachust design allowed the bottom parachute to open during balloon ascent and collection process. The top parachute and nylon line remain in the deployment bag until the payload has separated from the balloon. At that time, the deployed parachute descends to a point where the retrieval aircraft recovers the payload with a hook-and-line assembly which reels the recovered airman safely aboard the aircraft.

Balloon system during inflation. Bubble (foreground) is released from spool and ascends over payload (background) which is then released. Red wrap is for handling protection. Deployed parachute is part of flight train.

((NASA Wallops Flight Center)

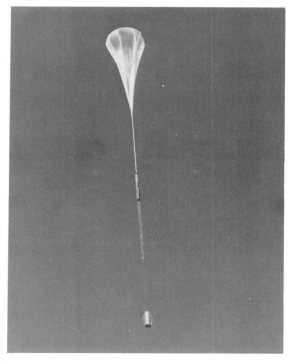

(b) The GHOST Flights

The most promising concepts for gathering the needed wind data were the GHOST (Global Horizontal Sounding Techniques) and its French counterpart, called EOLE. Both approaches were based on using strong, plastic super-pressure balloons to trace air circulations patterns, by drifting with wind at constant density altitudes. Scientists agreed that a system of balloons electronically linked to weather satellites could provide extensive knowledge of global meteorology and could be used in improving world-wide weather forecasts.

The practicability of constant-level balloons floating with the wind and tracked by remote telemetry was first studied by U.S. Navy scientists in the Transonde Project from 1957 to 1959. In 1958, Vincent Lally

GHOST balloon and telemetry package in simulated launch situation. (NCAR Photo)

A Ghost balloon rises eerily over the Bonneville salt flats, as engineers of the National Center for Atmospheric Research test a new way of launching in wind. In a zippered bag, the helium-filled balloon is run down-wind on an open truck, until the truck is going faster than the wind. Then the bag is unzipped and the balloon pops into the air. The Ghost (for Global Horizontal Sounding Technique) is a new type of plastic weather balloon that floats at a constant level. Thousands of these balloons could be put up to gather weather data as they circle the globe. (NCAR Photo)

and Thomas Haig of the Air Force Cambridge Research Laboratories (AFCRL) proposed the GHOST concept based on new developments in electronics and materials technology. By 1961 NCAR had become the institution for the development of GHOST under Lally's direction. (In 1962, AFCRL set a flight duration record using a Mylar super-pressure sphere which stayed aloft for 30 days.)

The GHOST plan was to float several thousand super-pressure balloons in the atmosphere at any one time; grouping them at constant density levels. Dropouts would be continuously replaced. Eighty-eight balloons were sent up the first year starting in March 1966. Each super-pressure balloon was provided with a sensing device and transmitting system for gathering information on its position and other data. Balloon transmissions were transmitted to a NASA Nimbus-4 meteorological satellite, which in turn relayed them to ground stations. About this time Winzen Research was making great strides to keep up with the demands for higher float altitudes, by developing 30-47-million-cubic-foot polyethylene balloons. Also, Raven Industries was manufacturing large Mylar super-pressure spheres having higher load-carrying capabilities. One of these spheres launched by the NSBF carried 150 pounds twice around the world over a period of 36 days, at an altitude of 80,000 feet, in the southern hemisphere, during March 1973. Payloads of up to 5,000 pounds have since become part of routine launchings. (By 1974, an international balloon network of super-pressures circling the globe was commonplace.)

During the first 8 years of the GHOST program some 60 super-pressure balloons were produced, with diameters ranging from 30 to 71 feet, lifting 230 pounds, reaching altitudes of as high as 108,000 feet and staying aloft as long as 261 days.

The planned profile of the first, earth-circling super-pressure balloon launched with a scientific payload looked like this.

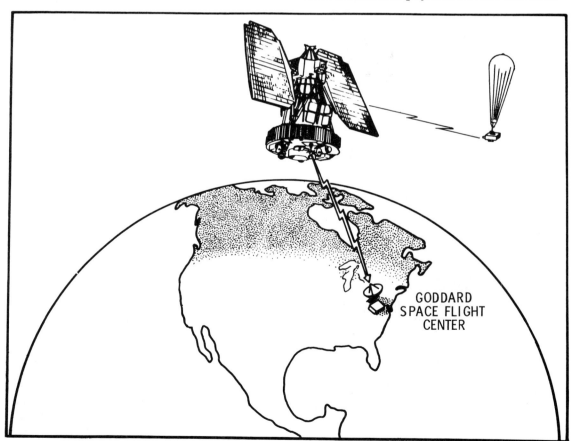

GODDARD
SPACE FLIGHT
CENTER

NASA and NCAR were conducting experiments in 1970 to get the location, pressure and temperature measurements at high altitudes using high-flying balloons by way of NASA's Nimbus-4 meteorological satellite. The balloons floated around the world at altitudes between 68,000 and 79,000 feet transmitting to Nimbus-4. Each balloon carried instruments called the Balloon Interrogation Package (BIP) while Nimbus-4 had a counterpart package called the Interrogation Recording and Location System (IRLS) which passed the data to earth.
(NASA Photo)

- 64-foot diameter sphere
- 137,300-cubic-foot volume
- Weight: 200 pounds
- Bilaminated polyester (0.002 inches)
- Designed to float 150 pounds of payload at 78,000 feet with a minimum altitude of 60,000 feet
- Launched at Oakey Air Field, Queensland, Australia
- Balloon floated at a constant-density altitude, moving in an east-to-west directional path ... Australia—Southern Africa—South America—Australia ... with an 18-day orbit running from January 24 to March 1, 1973

This balloon was launched just as described earlier, by utilizing a tow balloon to support the ballast. It made two orbits of the earth instead of one and on its way it conducted experiments studying cosmic rays and the effect of radiation on corn seedlings and other vegetatation; it also collected micrometeorites.

Future plans call for a non-laminated nylon pumpkin-shaped balloon, equipped with lightweight electronics and having a 500-pound payloard taken to an altitude of 130,000 feet, using a 300-foot diameter balloon.

In between May 27th and July 8th of 1970, 13 balloons were launched from the Ascension Islands to float around the world at altitudes from 68,999 to 79,000 feet. Each of these GHOST series balloons carried 10 pounds of instruments known as a BIP, or

Crews at NCAR's National Scientific Balloon Facility launched about 50 of these giant balloons each year for research scientists from around the world. This stratospheric research balloon was being launched from NCAR's National Scientific Balloon Facility (NSBF) at Palestine, Texas.
(NSBF Photo)

Balloon Interrogation Package.

High above, aboard the Nimbus-4 satellite, was a counterpart package called the Interrogation Recording and Location System (IRLS) which kept track of all the balloons. Programmed to activate every time it was in the transmitting area of one of the

Payload includes large sheets of photographic emulsion to be exposed by passage of cosmic-ray particles; a ballast hopper; telemetry; radio controls; and impact-absorbing crash pads (four boxes). *(National Scientific Balloon Facility)*

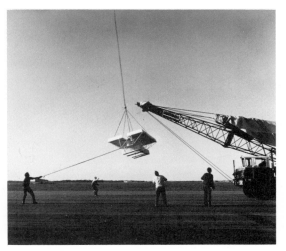

Payload is supported by a crane. Loadline, parachute and uninflated portion extend behind. A small "bubble" is inflated with helium which expands during ascent.
(NSBA Photo)

balloons, it sent a coded signal as the spacecraft passed over, requesting data from that particular balloon. The balloon recognizing the signal sent the data to Nimbus, which stored the information for later transmission to the ground.

After the conclusion of the Nimbus-4/IRLS flight program, in a joint NCAR, NASA and University of Wisconsin venture, a team proposed to test out the location and telemetry system to obtain data answering the question of how potential energy of the atmosphere can be converted into kinetic energy of atmospheric motion. Called TWERLE (Tropical Wind Energy Conversion and Reference Level Experiment), this program involved the launching of 400 instrumented, constant-level balloons into the atmosphere of the southern hemisphere during the year 1975. A Nimbus-6 satellite was the receiving end of the link. Each TWERLE balloon carried three sensors which measured altitude, temperature and pressure. A fourth parameter, the wind, was deduced from the balloon's position.

As an adjunct to the GARP plan, the global Atmospheric Measurements Program (GAMP) of 1968 was modified to include super-pressure balloons dropping radiosondes upon command to obtain needed tropical wind data. Under a NASA grant, NCAR conducted a 20-balloon series test, with each balloon carrying 64 dropsondes. Signals from the dropsondes were relayed to a mother balloon, then to the geostationary satellite for transmission to the ground station. The tests were completed in January 1971; the carrier balloon concept proving fruitful in obtaining weather data in the tropical troposphere.

For much of NASA's astronomical research balloons have provided an excellent platform to operate high in the atmosphere. Most large balloons are designed to fly higher than aircraft, operating above 100,000 feet and they can stay aloft from a few hours to many months. Balloons are also cheaper than satellites costing about $2,000 per million cubic feet and therefore, usually running from $10,000 to $80,000 each. Of course, balloons have become more costly as they have grown in size, as payloads have increased and as higher altitudes have been attempted.

(c) The Stratoscope Project

One of the more notable ventures of the

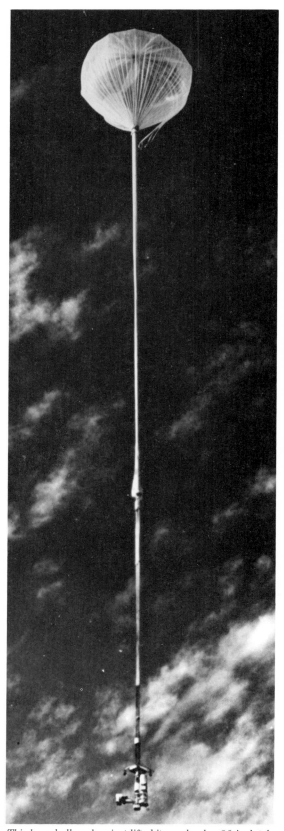

This huge balloon has just lifted its payload, a 36-inch telescope from the ground. The helium filled balloon will expand to a much larger size when it reaches altitude. Programmed for an 80,000 foot ceiling, it will analyze the infrared range of wave lengths from Mars. (NASA Photo)

STRATOSCOPE II
BALLOON SYSTEM CHARACTERISTICS

INFLATION TUBES

LAUNCH BALLOON

GAS-TRANSFER DUCT

59'

3'

210'

MAIN BALLOON

50' PARACHUTES

BALLOON CONTROL INSTRUMENTATION

105' SUSPENSION LINES AND RISERS

30' TELESCOPE ANTENNA SECTION

25' TELESCOPE

BALLOON SYSTEM AT 80,000 FT.

LAUNCH BALLOON
MATERIAL : GT–12
.5 MIL MYLAR
DACRON SCRIM (4 x 6 STRANDS / INCH)
TENSILE STRENGTH 36 LBS. / INCH
TYPE BALLOON: FULL SUPERPRESSURE CYLINDER
VOLUME : 305,000 FT^3

MAIN BALLOON
MATERIAL: GT–11
.35 MIL MYLAR
DACRON SCRIM (4 x 6 STRANDS / INCH)
TYPE BALLOON: TAILORED NATURAL SHAPE
VOLUME : 5,250,000 FT.^{3}

LENGTH OVERALL
AT LAUNCH : 660 FT.   AT 80,000 FT. : 480 FT.

WEIGHT
PAYLOAD : 7350 LBS.   OVERALL : 14500 LBS.

GROSS LIFT : 16000 LBS.

FREE LIFT : 1500 LBS.

Artist concept of the Stratoscope II Balloon System. The tandem balloons with the 36 inch telescope was launched from Palestine, Texas to an altitude of some 15 miles. Photographs were made through the telescope of the planet Jupiter and other distant celestial objects.
(NASA Photo)

During the Stratoscope I flights over 400 photographs of sunspots were taken which did lead to a better understanding of the motions observed in the strong magnetic fields of the sunspots. The telescope-camera was equipped with a closed circuit television camera and remote control mechanism that enabled the research team to guide the camera and see on the TV screen the area under observation.
(NCAR/NSF Photo)

This sequence of photographs was taken during the launch of a typical scientific experiment under the Skyhook program in 1972 and shows experimental equipment for the balloon hanging from the launch truck boom, the balloon bubble being inflated with helium gas, immediately after being released from the anchor vehicle, and momentarily suspended over the launch vehicle just before picking up the payload. In the last photograph, the balloon has been launched and is ascending toward its float altitude. *(NCAR/NSF Photo)*

Four plastic Skyhook balloons, constructed for the ONR by General Mills, Inc., are prepared for an early morning launch. The Skyhooks appear only partially inflated because the gas expands as the balloons rise to the upper atmosphere.
(U.S. Navy Photo)

Skyhook balloon 93 leaving the deck of the U.S.S. Norton Sound.
(U.S. Navy Photo)

In the foreground is the parachute which will return the payload of scientific instruments to the ground. The stratospheric research balloon in the background will carry its cargo on a predetermined flight path above the earth.

(NCAR/NSF Photo)

An NCAR technician at the National Scientific Balloon Facility removes the protective covering from the actual balloon train just prior to launch. *(NCAR/NSF Photo)*

A giant spool holds a balloon down as the bubble—the portion of the balloon filled with helium for launching—expands and rises. On the ground, the balloons are only partially inflated. As they rise into a less dense atmosphere, the helium in the balloon expands sometimes to a size large enough to encompass a football stadium or two. *(NCAR/NSF Photo)*

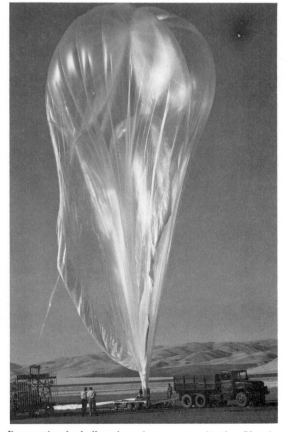

Preparation for balloon launch. *(Author Photo)*

35

early '60s was the Stratoscope II flights. Through the cooperation and joint sponsorship of the National Science Foundation, the U.S. Navy and NASA, numerous aerospace programs have been developed through NCAR. The Stratoscope II program was one of these. It involved the repeated launching and retrieval of a 3½-ton astronomical observatory which was designed to obtain high resolution celestial photos more detailed than an earthbound telescope could produce. The balloon-borne telescope has transmitted back a variety of infrared spectral data on the Moon, Mars, certain cool Red Giant stars and many other space phenomena. The Stratoscope series milestones go back to 1947 with the beginning of the Navy's Skyhook program. Stratoscope's explorations have resulted in revising the current astronomical theories on the evolution and structure of the stars and the characteristics of the planets.

Starting in January, 1960, a new series of Skyhook balloon flights were underway. The size of these balloons ranged upward to 10 million cubic feet, with a thickness of 0.001-inch thick polyethylene. Some of these balloons reached altitudes of 120,000 feet with 2,500-pound payloads of cosmic-ray research equipment.

(d) The Echo Series

This same year, NASA used a missile to launch a 100-foot-diameter, aluminum-coated, spherical balloon into space. Named Echo I, this novel balloon went into near circular orbit about 1,000 miles above the earth. This spectacular inflatable device be-

X-ray telescope preparatory to the launch of a balloon from Australia in April 1972; and after launch.

(NCAR/NSF Photo)

The 42-foot, 52-ton balloon launch vehicle (nicknamed Tiny Tim) was built to order for NCAR by R. G. LeTourneau, Inc., Longview, Texas. It holds heavy scientific instruments suspended while a balloon is being inflated, then moves downwind to release the payload as the balloon rises above the vehicle.

(NCAR/ARF Photo)

Echo II stage four of inflations.   (NASA Photo)

across the continent and from the United States to Europe.

The most famous unmanned satellite to be launched by NASA was undoubtedly ECHO I, the 100-foot inflatable, spherical communications balloon. Following its launch from Cape Canaveral, August 12, 1960, it was to remain in orbit and visible in the night sky for more than 8 years. Lesser known were the smaller inflatable spheres, forerunners to ECHO, all a part of the PARD project conducted by NASA scientist W.J. O'Sullivan, Jr.

The series of inflatable spheres for space was first proposed by O'Sullivan in the mid-50's, followed by the first test at Wallops Center of a 30-inch inflatable sphere made of aluminum foil laminated with Mylar film on both sides of it. This was followed in the same year, 1958, with flight tests being made with the complete three-stage Nike-Cajun-Little David test vehicle, Vanguard and a Jupiter C rocket.

Two solar-powered radio beacons were carried aboard Echo I to assist in tracking and locating the satellite.

Expected to stay up a year, Echo I lasted eight years and logged more than one billion miles! Gradually, its skin bombarded by micrometeorites and space dust, its gas leaked and it became wrinkled as a prune. Inexorably, pushed by solar winds and pulled by gravity, Echo I fell back into the atmosphere where it burned off the west coast of South America during the evening of June 23, 1968.

The succeeding Echo II was designed to specifications more than 50 times as strong as Echo I. This second and larger balloon satellite was placed into orbit in 1964.

The Echo series has also provided valuable technical and operational data on the actual mechanisms by which radiation and solar particles heat up the atmosphere and has paved the way in the development of large, erectable satellites.

Following the Echo I and II, a new wire-grid style was introduced. This was also a passive satellite. Launched into a 545-nautical-mile orbit, this type inflated to its 30-foot spherical shape, whereupon, its filmy skin photolyzed...disintegrating, to leave an open mesh screen of wire element with ⅙-inch wide spaces. In this form, it remained rigid and proved an excellent reflector of space radio waves. It was technology such as this that prepared the way for to-

came the first passive communication satellite of its kind against which voice, picture and music were able to be bounced from one part of the United States to another.

The ½-mil. Mylar balloon, coated with aluminum, was folded into a 26½-inch magnesium sphere fitted to the nose of a Delta rocket. The container was split open by an explosive charge and the balloon quickly inflated through the use of a sublimating material. Then, as the satellite became warmed by the Sun, certain chemicals, also within, vaporized, and so maintained the inflated shape.

In orbit, NASA's first communications satellite sparkled brighter than the North Star in the evening and predawn skies, as it passed over most of the Earth's populated areas. As the most visible evidence of the U.S. space program, the big, bright balloon caught the imagination of millions around the world.

Circling the globe every two hours, Echo served as a passive "mirror in space," reflecting signals beamed to it from the ground over intercontinental distances. Its first transmission proved typically American . . . "This is President Eisenhower speaking. The satellite balloon which has reflected these words may be used freely by any nation for similar experiments in their own interests." In the weeks and months that followed, Echo I relayed voices, music, pictures, facsimile letters and teletype signals

A four stage Scout rocket launched from Wallops, is shown at lift-off. The twelve foot diameter inflatable sphere was an experiment to determine atmospheric density at various altitudes. (NASA Photo)

day's worldwide communications and navigation systems.

With the space program underway, it soon became evident that accurate density data was needed of the space region around the earth. It was decided to place a low mass, high-area ratio satellite into an eccentric orbit to examine this zone. The Explorer IX satellite was designed specifically for this purpose. The 12-foot diameter plastic and aluminum foil balloon, printed with white polka dots, weighted only 15 pounds, yet was sturdy enough to remain spherical at the edge of the near-space environment. Explorer IX was launched on February 16, 1961 from the Wallops Flight Center by a solid-propellant Scout vehicle. It established an orbit with maximum altitude of 395 statute miles. The shiny metallic surface of Explorer IX permitted both radar and optical tracking.

The Explorer IX remained in orbit many years, providing new data on air density, solar radiation, pressure and a new phenomenon called the "hellium bulge."

Several other inflatable satellites launched during this period were the Project Able and PAGEOS balloons.

The purpose of the satellite in Project Able was to reflect the Sun's light and illuminate specific areas on the earth's surface during nighttime hours for periods of up to six months or more. The Goodyear Corporation was the contractor of the project and their design parameters were to create a 1,500- to 3,000-foot diameter reflector based on an inflatable, torus and truss configurations. A film, or wire-grid, composite material was to be used so that it could be packaged into a random shape or form.

Echo I has last minute check on payload. (NASA Photo)

A scientist examined the flight package of a 100-foot sphere, which was part of the inflatable satellite program of NASA. The sphere was launched into space in a relatively small package and inflated automatically in space. It has potential application also as a lunar probe. (NASA Photo)

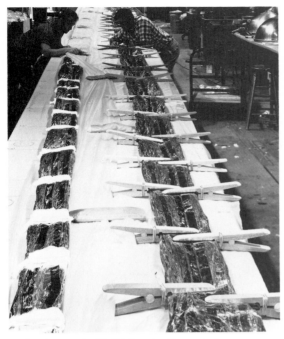

Technicians at the NASA Langley Research Center prepare two micro-thin aluminium-coated plastic satellites for future journeys into space. Each satellite is slightly more than 157 feet long. They will be compactly folded into metal payload containers 26½ inches in diameter. The satellite at right is in the early stages of folding and is held in place by 12-inch clothespins. The satellite at left, further along in the intricate folding process, is being encased in a vinyl sleeve preparatory to the evacuation of bulk air trapped inside. After the satellite is placed in its container, the remaining air is forced out through 242 pin holes made in the plastic space vehicle during folding. (NASA Photo)

The inflatable space structure was to be steerable to a very fine degree so that illumination could be maintained during the continually changing earth-sun-satellite relationship. The large surface of the reflector was to have extremely smooth, flat faces so that control of the size and illumination level of the spot on earth was very precise.

In an effort to develop measurements of the size and shape of the earth and its gravity field that would be of an accuracy far beyond what had come before, the National Geodetic Satellite Program was initiated. NASA was given charge. The vehicle used for this worldwide data acquisition was called PAGEOS (Passive Geodetic Earth Orbiting Satellite). The satellite itself was an inflatable, aluminized Mylar of highly reflective surface with a coating to protect it from ultraviolet radiation. To fabricate the balloon, it took gores 45 inches wide at the center and 157 feet long. (In a 1965 report to NASA, Goodyear Aerospace presented results of a test for reflectivity of a passive

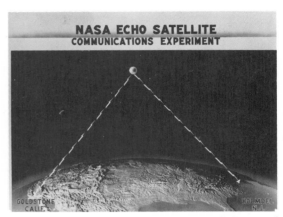

Echo I satellite, a 100-foot diameter inflatable balloon used as a passive communications space satellite. (NASA Photo)

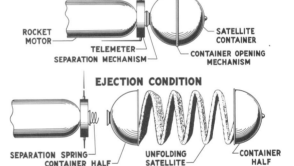

Launch and ejection sequence of 100-foot inflatable sphere in Project Echo. Container separates from burnt out third stage on injection into orbit. (NASA Photo)

Inflated Echo I sphere. (NASA Photo)

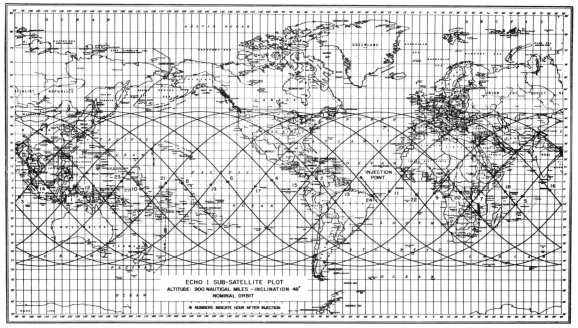

Orbital plot of Echo I satellite. (NASA Photo)

communications satellite. The model used was five feet in diameter and was to determine materials and types of gore seams to be used in future designs. Goodyear concluded that conducive, overlapping seams were the most efficient for this type of satellite.)

Echo I telemetry checkout on payload. (NASA Photo)

The seams of the PAGEOS satellite were butted together and sealed with a one-inch wide tape made from the same material as that used for the gores. Before the last gore was sealed and pleat-folded, 168 reinforced vent holes were evenly spaced along a meridian which circumscribed the sphere along its outer side. The sublimating compound was evenly distributed between the folds. Finally, the last gore was sealed and the sphere was folded in a rotated "accordion" pattern and packaged into the cannister.

Launched from the U.S. western test range on June 23, 1966, the space craft was carried into orbit on a Thor-Agena D vehicle; a two-stage thrust-augmented rocket. Upon climbing to approximately 2,295 nautical miles, the craft went into orbit. The cannister was spring-ejected from the second stage at a low velocity. Achieving a separation distance of 500 feet, a pyrotechnic device separated the cannister halves and allowed the folded sphere to be inflated. PAGEOS was off on its 5-year mission.

(e) Miscellaneous Achievements

On August 16, 1960, Captain Kittinger bettered his own and any previous record by reaching higher than any man had risen in a non-powered flight. He ascended in an open basket beneath a 400-foot balloon made of Mylar to a height of 102,800 feet. He then parachuted to earth. This all was part of a

40

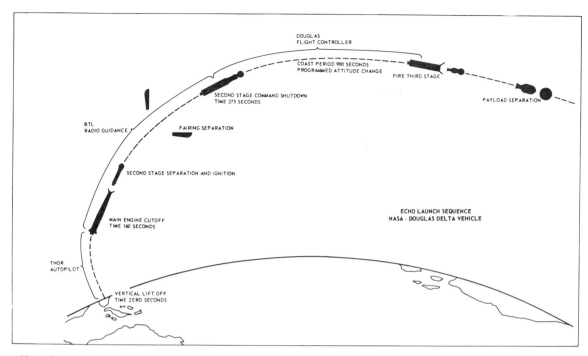

Chart shows performance of Delta launch vehicle in ejecting into orbit a project Echo I passive communications satellite.
(NASA Photo)

(NASA Photo)

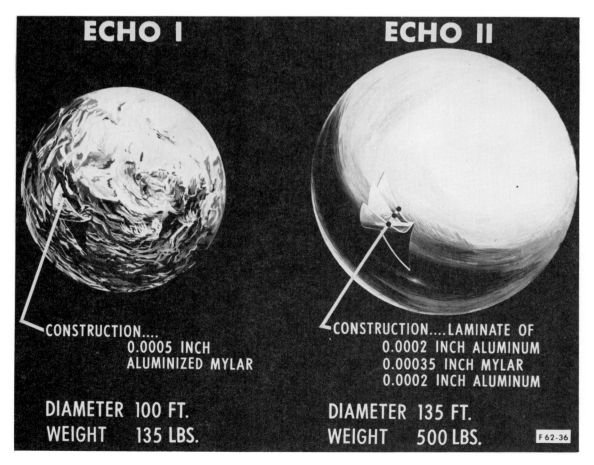

Scientists at NASA's Langley Research Center complete the first ground inflation tests of a 135-foot-diameter inflatable spherical satellite. Purpose of the ground test is to verify the structural strength of the sphere. The rigidized sphere is thicker and heavier than Echo I and is designed as the prototype of passive communications satellites of the future. *(NASA Photo)*

NASA scientists use a 30-inch scale version of an inflatable 135-foot diameter sphere in their High Vacuum Facility during general research. *(NASA Photo)*

(NASA Photo)

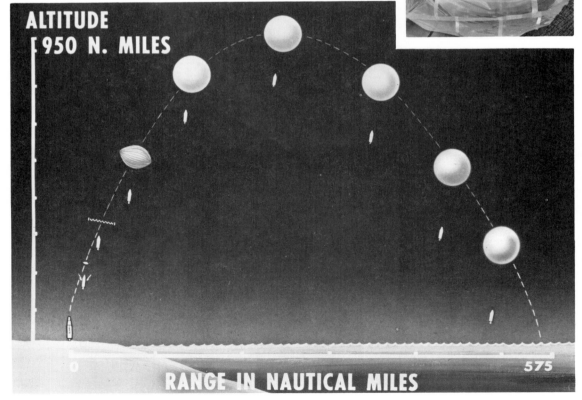

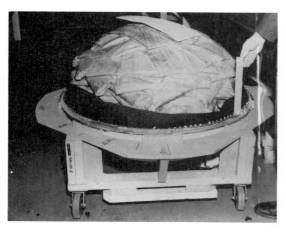

The canister in which the Echo II Satelloon was folded had an oblate spheriod design about a tenth of an inch thick. It was folded with an accordian pleat into one of two flanged half-shelled canisters. *(Schjeldahl Photo)*

Technician examines a 40-inch metal payload container for an inflatable sphere of the Echo II passive communications satellite type. *(NASA Photo)*

Echo Communications Satellite Series
The 135 foot design of Echo II stems basically from spherical pressure balloons. Containing about 1,000 square yards of material, made of 106 gores that are four feet wide at the equator and tapering to the points of attachment. Echo II was packed uninflated in an 11 cubic foot column canister . . . a ratio of 100,000 to 1. The sandwich material, capable of self-rigidizing in space, is a laminate with a precise combination of cold rolled aluminum foil and DuPont Mylar.

Inflation ducts on ground test model of Echo II.
(Schjeldahl Photo)

Inflated Echo II shows panels and size in hangar.
(Schjeldahl Photo)

NASA conducted an inflation test on Echo II, the second passive communications satellite. The 135-foot diameter sphere underwent radio frequency reflectivity characteristics tests as well as its degree of sphericity at varying levels of inflation pressure.

(NASA Photo)

study on earth-return, gathering information for future space flights.

During the same month a balloon parachute combination was tested for use in the recovery of missiles. The 9-foot fabric-coated balloon which could inflate in one-tenth of a second, was designed to control the deceleration and tumbling effects of a re-entering space vehicle until it reached a lower altitude where the parachute could take over.

Eight months later, on May 4, 1961, Commander Ross of the U.S. Navy, piloted to a record height of 113,500 feet in a 10-million-cubic-foot Strato-Lab balloon, thus setting a new altitude record. The open cage-like gondola made of aluminum tubing was launched from an aircraft carrier over the Gulf of Mexico. The two men in the crew were protected from the near space environment by only their pressure suits and a modified set of household venetian blinds installed on the gondola.

In 1961, Raven Industries designed a one-man thermal balloon called Vulcoon, which was used for sport and commercial activities. The 30,000-cubic-foot hot air

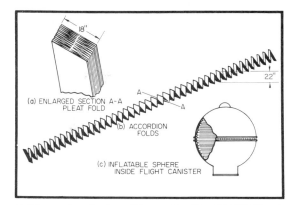

Folding and packaging of Pageos Satellite. (NASA Photo)

envelope had a 40-foot diameter and stood 50 feet high when inflated for take-off. The Vulcoon carried a payload of 240 pounds, which included a pilot and parachute, and a full tank of fuel. Without an oxygen supply, the top safe altitude was 12,000 feet.

On July 23, 1961, the Free Clinic Relief Association reported from Taipei that it used balloons to deliver food parcels as far as 1,000 miles into the interior of mainland China.

In 1962, small, low-flying balloons filled with just enough helium to allow them to

Inflated Pageos (Passive Geodetic Earth-Orbiting Satellite) Satelloon.   *(Schjeldahl Photo)*

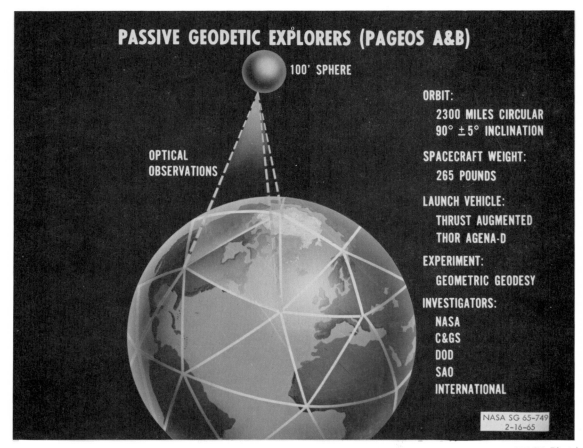

PASSIVE GEODETIC EXPLORERS (PAGEOS A&B)

100' SPHERE

OPTICAL OBSERVATIONS

ORBIT:
2300 MILES CIRCULAR
90° ± 5° INCLINATION

SPACECRAFT WEIGHT:
265 POUNDS

LAUNCH VEHICLE:
THRUST AUGMENTED
THOR AGENA-D

EXPERIMENT:
GEOMETRIC GEODESY

INVESTIGATORS:
NASA
C&GS
DOD
SAO
INTERNATIONAL

NASA SG 65-749
2-16-65

(NASA Photo)

rise slowly above the ground, were being used to track down environmentally unpleasant odors and air pollution in industrialized areas. New York City released 50 tetrahedrally-shaped balloons, five feet on each side, to examine air pollution.

A Soviet-built balloon with 24 pieces of cardboard covered with tinfoil hanging from it was reported by the Japanese on May 6, 1962. The balloon was tracked across western Honshu, the main Japanese island, until it landed off Shima Peninsula in the ocean 300 miles southwest of Tokyo.

In September, 1967, a Soviet news agency reported that Soviet engineers were working on a balloon-borne power station to tap the power of the wind five or six miles up. The Soviet project envisaged a wind wheel mounted on a balloon 725 feet long and 132 feet in diameter. The envelope had three layers lined with glass plastics and filled with foam plastics. The report revealed also a balloon-supported windmill whose power was fed through a control system and a step-down transformer to the ground. This design was also being considered as a relay for radio and television.

From Toronto, Canada, 1,000 meteorological balloons were released in October, 1966, to trace air pollution. Two hundred were found eventually near such areas as Wilmington, Delaware, and Quebec City and Gravenhorst, Ontario.

Of particular interest to the world scientific community has been the work of an international organization called SPARMO (Solar Particles and Radiation Monitoring Organization) which was created in 1961 at Paris. It later changed its name to SBARMO (Scientific Ballooning and Radiations Monitoring Organization). SBARMO has been coordinating balloon recordings of solar particle radiation, and more recently, been recording auroral-zone and the x-ray events associated with the precipitation of high energy electrons. The international organization has been furthering the standardization of aerospace equipment, the development of safety rules for scientific balloon flights and has focused on technical problems allied to stratospheric balloon flights.

On December 10, 1963, Raven Industries reported its participation in a study of the north polar region. The 1.5-million-

From left to right, LCDR Lee M. Lewis, Charles Moore, and LCDR Malcolm D. Ross prepare to enter the gondola for a test of the equipment used in Project Stratolab IV. *(Official U.S. Navy Photo)*

cubic-foot, Raven-built balloon was to lift off from Point Barrow, Alaska, to an altitude of 100,000 feet, carrying equipment to measure cosmic rays, polar radio blackout conditions, ozone distribution, electric field gradient, auroral displays and the fluctuations in the Van Allen belts. The program, called Polar Circling Balloon Observatory, was part of an 18-month geophysical study by scientists from many nations conducted during this period of maximum solar activities (flares and sunspots).

On that same day, the National Science Foundation, the sponsor of the project, pro-vided a grant to the University of Minnesota for a minimum of twenty 1.5-million-cubic-foot plastic balloons to be launched from Point Barrow. Under the two-year project headed by Dr. John R. Winkler, a space physicist and cosmic ray expert, each balloon would carry 45 pounds of instruments to explore the upper atmosphere and the phenomena of aurora borealis. Each balloon suspended a 6,000-foot radio antenna to transmit on the low frequency of 70 kilocycles, radio signals over the curvature of the earth.

NASA's Marshall Space Flight Center

CDR Malcolm D. Ross getting into his space suit aboard USS Antietam for Strato Lab High No. 5.
(Official U.S. Navy Photo)

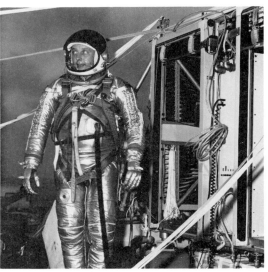

LCDR Victor A. Prather, suited and waiting to enter gondola. (Official U.S. Navy Photo)

Prather and Ross in gondola aboard USS Antietam prior to Strato High Lab launching. Aerial view of ship with balloon on deck during inflation and lift-off.
(Official U.S. Navy Photo)

in Alabama repoirted in August, 1964, that G.T. Schjeldahl Company was contracted to manufacture a meteorological balloon with "warts" raised on its surface to make the aerostat more stable in turbulent air streams than it would experience with smooth, spherical balloons.

On May 30, 1965, two 100,000-cubic-foot balloons were launched from the schooner, Goodwill, off the Cook Islands, carrying the University of Minnesota's scientific equipment to the upper atmosphere to examine the sun's eclipse.

Another record balloon flight was made on February 2, 1966, from Sioux Falls, South Dakota, by Nicholas Piantanida to an altitude of 123,500 feet, well above the record held by Ross and Prather. Piantanida intended to break another record by a free-fall parachute jump. When he first disconnected his line from the tank in the gondola and attempted to hook it up to the tank on his back, he found the coupling was frozen and could not be released. Piantanida had to

give up and request the controller on the ground to release the gondola from the balloon by radio signal. He then fell 5 miles to 97,000 feet before the gondola's parachute opened. Piantanida fortunately returned to earth safely, but because the balloon did not return to earth with him, the FAI did not recognize the altitude as a record.

By 1970, scientific payloads were being balloon-carried to altitudes above 99.8% of the earth's atmosphere. During the course of a yearly period the United States was launching over 500 high-altitude, constant-level balloons. Manned and unmanned balloons were engaged in aeronomy, solar physics, astronomy, energetic particle research, magnetic fields, micrometerites and cosmic dust, planetary observations, biology, visible light particle sampling and pressure-temperature sensing. At the same time, industry and government were improving balloon reliability and technology in areas of launch, flight, inflation shelters, and balloon materials.

Final check of an air-sampling payload before launch by USAF personnel from Holloman AFB, New Mexico. The samplers are designed to collect stratospheric dust particles at altitudes from 60,000 to 120,000 feet.   *(USAF Photo)*

Preparing inflatable spheres for space flight. (NASA Photo)

Balloon used to carry animal and micro-biological experiments prior to takeoff at Goose Bay, Labrador.
(NASA Photo)

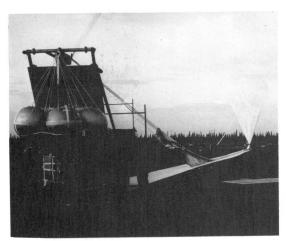

The balloon payload consists of four capsules.
(NASA Photo)

Four recovered strapped capsules are shown in heavily wooded area of Canada after being cut down.
(NASA Photo)

Retrieval of a payload returned to earth.
(NCAR/NSF Photo)

Close-up of monkeys in their capsule couches immediately after recovery. The boxes in front of monkeys are food containers.
(NASA Photo)

(f) Powered Balloons

Beginning in the late 1960's, several government agencies contracting through private industry undertook the development of manned and unmanned powered balloons to be used for scientific experimentation and military operations. The results were promising.

High Platform I was one of the earliest attempts and involved Goodyear Aerospace and Winzen Research. The concept was to power an unmanned balloon at high altitudes. A free balloon was thus maintained on station in the upper atmosphere, powered by a silicon-solar array driving an electric propeller.

Early in 1969, High Platform II began development under the auspices of Raven Industries. This unique 136-pound aerostat proved itself capable of operating for an extended period greater than six months at an altitude of 70,000 feet. This powered super-pressure balloon had a fineness ratio of 3:1 and was completely sealed—it's envelope being made of bilaminate Mylar. Solar cells provided the power source for driving the light, molded propeller at a designed speed of 20 knots. The control surfaces attached to the hull included a vertical stationary fin, a rudder, two horizontal stabilizers and two elevators. The gondola of High Platform II provided the support for the mechanical components of the propulsion system. An

This experimental powered balloon was flown successfully at 70,000 feet altitude. It was solar powered. (Note photo cell array on nose.)

(Raven Industries)

anemometer was suspended beneath it. Test flights during 1970 proved the feasibility of this design.

POBAL, or powered balloon, was an U.S. Air Force program started in 1969 under a contract with Goodyear to test out the stationkeeping capability of a powered balloon remotely controlled at high altitudes. Both streamlined and natural-shaped designs were looked into, configured with reciprocating engines, turbines and electric motors as candidates for possible power supply and with fuel cells, solar cells and batteries as possible power sources. As conceived, this powered polyethylene balloon was larger, heavier and more powerful than High Platform I. In September 1972, POBAL carried a 4,000-pound payload to 60,000 feet. In this particular configuration, 2,000 pounds were taken up by silver-zinc batteries that powered an electric motor which in turn drove a 35-foot helicopter rotor at 200 rpm. A rudder located in the slipstream of the propeller controlled the direction of the motor thrust.

Another POBAL design, this one developed by Raven Industries, used fuel cells rather than batteries and was launched tail first using a tow balloon and crane. It was a system obviously designed for comparing operational data with the Goodyear design.

One military-applied design by Schjeldahl Company made use of two 3 hp McCulloch chainsaw motors for its propulsion. These were later replaced with battery powered electric motors, attaining a maximum flight speed of 12 knots. Steering was accomplished by varying the speed of either outboard engine. The name of the project was Silent Joe I. In a follow-up project, called Silent Joe II, a propulsion unit was added to the stern of the craft consisting of a propeller driven by a hydraulic motor. These devices were used over Southeast Asia. With remotely controlled flight path, these little drones carried microphones and a radio transreceiver, and were capable of detecting enemy truck convoys and troop movements with radar. Nine flights were reported in 1968 and '69.

Microblimp was yet another powered type. Built by Raven Industries, this vehicle had a class C-shaped hull and a fineness ratio of 3:1. The craft had a cruising altitude of 5,000 feet and cruise speed of 30 knots. Microblimp's power came from a stern-mounted 4 hp Wankel engine driving an eight-foot diameter, molded polyurethane, three-bladed propeller. Directional control was achieved by gimbaling the engine-propeler assembly. Heading and pitch control were maintained by an autopilot. Radio-controlled, the Microblimp had a range of 5 miles and completed many flights.

High Platform III had a volume of 600,000 cubic feet and a fineness ratio of 5:1. This super-pressure balloon was designed for constant-level operations at an altitude of 85,000 feet. Completed in August 1971, it had some very interesting features such as fins pressurized by a small air compressor. Power to the motor was supplied by a solar array capable of providing an airspeed of 15 knots continuously, 24 hours a day, for four months.

Another comparable design completed in 1973 was the High Altitude Station Keeping Vehicle. Its mission was much the same as that for the High Platform III balloon.

The High Altitude Powered Platform (HAPP) was a concept for a remotely controlled, long-endurance platform combining the characteristics of zero-pressure and super-pressure balloons with those of an airship. A U.S. Navy project toward realizing this concept was the High Altitude Superpressure Powered Aerostat (HASPA). The mission of HASPA was to develop a surveillance vehicle capable of flying a 200-pound payload at an altitude of 70,000 feet for periods up to 30 days. On-board power was derived from several different sources; solar photo voltaic cells, fuel cells and batteries. Two electric motors produced 5 hp for driving the stern propeller. Launched in a limp state, the balloon filled as it rose and its helium expanded.

Enough commercial and military interest was shown for powered balloons that Raven Industries in 1974 embarked on the development of a manned, thermal, lighter-than-air craft. STAR (Small Thermal Airship) was the result. It was an aerodynamically-shaped, powered, hot air balloon. By January 1975, it had completed its maiden voyage. The 140,000-cubic-foot STAR had a speed of 25 mph, a duration of three hours and a useful lift of 500 pounds.

The STAR balloon used hot air generated by an on-board propane burner. By regulating the use of its burner, altitude control was achieved; thus the burner was its buoyancy medium. A 65 hp fan kept the airship pressurized. Its service ceiling was 4,000

Inflataplane package, laid out for inflation and completely assembled and inflated. Research ordered by the Office of Naval Research and built by Goodyear Aerospace.

(Goodyear Photo)

A 50-foot long Rogallo paraglider model with inflated fabric tubes is being towed to altitude for tests. The paraglider is released in free-flight glides to determine its flight behavior, load carrying capability, and landing characteristics.

(NASA Photo)

feet and its gross load was 2,030 pounds, including 78 gallons of propane. The payload was 100 pounds.

The STAR could be transported on a medium truck to any take-off site where the primary assembly work involved attaching the gondola to the balloon. Deflation was achieved through the use of a pull-out panel just as used on present-day hot air balloons.

Remotely controlled low altitude aerostat. Built to demonstrate several design concepts. *(Raven Industries)*

The Starship Enterprise became operational in 1975 as a manned, thermal lighter-than-air craft. *(Raven Industries)*

(g) Tethered Balloons

Along with developments in powered balloons, developments in tethered balloons also advanced during the early '70s. The shapes of tethered balloons are usually divided into three categories: spherical, natural shape and aerodynamic shape (a single hull or a double intersecting hull like the Vee-Balloon).

The first two shapes are the earliest types and provide the greater volumetric efficiency. The natural shape is more efficient from a structural standpoint. Both of these shapes are widely used as free balloons but are limited in tethered applications. The natural-shape, free balloon normally vented by an appendix, has no pressurization other than the head of lifting gas in the envelope.

When tethered, any balloon, regardless of configuration, will have an externally-applied pressure on the windward side. This impact is called dimpling, or "cupping," unless the balloon has a greater internal pressure.

Aerodynamically-shaped balloons were the response for replacing the high drag and instability of the early spherical balloons with their wind limitations. The natural-shaped aerostat has the greatest drag in wind; a spherical balloon, lesser drag; and the aerodynamic balloon, the least drag. The aerodynamically-shaped balloon is inherently heavier, for a given volume, than spherical or natural-shaped balloons but is capable of operating in higher wind velocities. The Vee-Balloon is such a type.

Goodyear developed the Vee-Balloon for

Use of calcium light from balloon to illuminate movements of troops during Civil War. Experiment made by Prof. Lowe.
(Smithsonian Institute)

Photo is a scene in making the movie "Five Weeks in a Balloon." Observation balloon like this type used in World War I. *(University of Akron Archives Photo)*

Barrage balloon, May, 1940.
(University of Akron Archives Photo)

54

VEE-BALLOON—This inflatable structure was developed by Goodyear Aircraft Corporation in the early 1960's for supporting scientific instruments above the ground. The company later constructed four 110-foot long "Vee-Balloons" under a contract from General Electric Company, Syracuse. Inflated with helium, the structures are tethered to the ground and can hold equipment aloft for extended periods in almost any weather. (Goodyear Photo)

This USAF aerodynamically shaped tethered balloon has a volume of 70,000 cubic feet. The tether cable is made of Kevlar, which has a strength-to-weight ratio three times as great as 1/4" steel cable. (USAF Photo)

Balloons with instrumentation packages are used to gather data near Rattlesnake Mountain for a DOE-sponsored study of night winds. Helium gives shape to the balloon, held by project manager Thomas W. Horst, a Battelle scientist. (U.S. Department of Energy)

Goodyear tethered balloon in hangar, 1941. (Goodyear Photo)

supporting scientific instruments for logistics, surveillance, and commercial operations above ground. The 110-foot long, inflatable fabric structure held equipment aloft for extended periods in almost all weather conditions. It resembled two huge silver cigars, 28 feet in diameter, fused together at one end at a 40-degree angle. The 75,000-cubic-foot helium-filled Vee-Balloon contained automatic dilative devices for maintaining the gas pressure at different altitudes and temperatures. The new dacron fabric used was five times more impermeable to gases than coated fabric, with a strength/weight ratio two to six times greater than the unsupported films used in high altitude balloons.

A high-altitude, tethered balloon was designed, having a streamlined lower balloon at about 20,000 feet and a natural-shape balloon at the 60,000-foot altitude. The British *New Scientist* on November 8, 1973, reported the use of a 250,000-cubic-foot tethered balloon of this type, supporting 3,500 pounds of equipment, relaying television programs to the Bahamas at altitudes between 10,000 to 15,000 feet.

Both zero-pressure and super-pressure, natural-shaped envelopes have been used in tethered operations. Oceanographer Phillipe Cousteau has used the 40-foot, zero-pressure model with his laboratory vessel, Calypso. The tuna industry have used hot air balloons as work platforms for aerial fish spotting.

During 1973 and 1974, the Advanced Research Project Agency (ARPA) of the Department of Defense, working with NASA and the Schjeldahl Corporation, used the Cape Canaveral Air Force station to test its Family II Tethered Balloon System. This design lifted a 750-pound payload to 12,000 feet. Its main application is Heavy Lift Station Keeping, but the range of promising uses of tethered balloons is quite extensive. These include:

- Acoustic Surveillance: to detect enemy site locations, troop and vehicle movements.
- Radar Surveillance and Detection: to seal off the U.S. borders from illegal entrants.
- Optical Surveillance: for general battlefield reconnaisance and defense perimeter control against infiltration and encroachment.
- Communications Relay: for point-to-point relay or area broadcasting; span-

ning very long distances or covering very large areas.

- Navigation and Antenna Elevation: to elevate an antenna weighing several tons to a moderate altitude; and by using a balloon-borne relay, locate the position of airborne and ground vehicles.

- Transport: to on- or off-load container-ships, without the use of dock facilities. As a balloon logistical support facility: a container is attached to a balloon, lifted up, and then both the container and the balloon are pulled to the shore or ship by cable winch.

In March 1973, at a test site in Oregon, a logging balloon was used by the Department of Defense to airlift cargo from ships to military beachheads. This 530,000 cubic foot balloon was built by Raven Industries.

Ground support systems are also undergoing development to keep pace, particularly with the diverse types and sizes of tethered, lighter-than-air vehicles. William C. Lane of Otis Engineering Corporation revealed the development of a high-speed, automatic inhaul winch system for the U.S. Air Force that prevents slack in the lines of

This Soviet balloon is capable of being used as a telemeter; for meteorological research; as a communication antenna; or for radar transmission. (Official U.S. Navy Photo)

The Hugo I system.
(NCAR/NSF Photo)

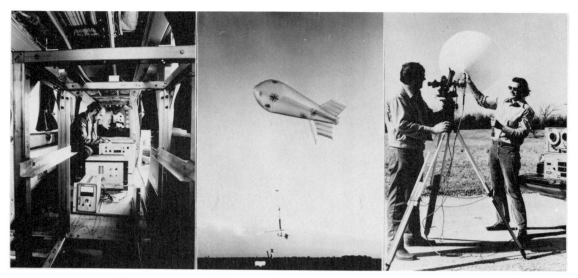

Multistate Atmospheric Power Production (MAP) Study, investigated the atmospheric behavior of air pollutants generated by the burning of coal. (Photos left to right). Scientists install sophisticated air pollution monitoring equipment in aircraft. At dusk, a tethered balloon is prepared to carry a package of sensitive meteorological equipment aloft. Researcher from Argonne prepares to release and track a small balloon containing a miniature instrument used to measure wind, height and temperature.

(BNL & ANL Photos)

The Aerocrane combines a free balloon with rotors, having many possible applications, among them moving cargo from ship-to-shore.

(Official U.S. Navy Photo)

58

One of the first successful logging operations using a helium balloon to lift and carry the logs down the mountain. This 240,000 cubic foot prototype was followed by operational balloons with volumes of 530,000 cubic feet and larger.   (Raven Industries Photo)

This diagram shows the balloon system in three operating positions on a typical overstory removal operation.

HOW THE SYSTEM WORKS

1. *Balloon has been pulled up the hill by the haulback line and its own lift. When over its destination, the balloon is pulled to the ground by tightening the haulback line. Loggers secure chokers around the logs.*

2. *Balloon gains height as haulback line is slackened. Mainline is pulled in, drawing balloon toward the landing.*

3. *Balloon deposits "turn" of logs at the landing as mainline is again tightened.*   (Raven Industries Photo)

tethered balloon systems. Automatic inhaul begins when the line tension drops below a preselected actuated tension. The winch accelerates whenever it needs to maintain proper tension. Inhaul ceases as line tension returns to an acceptable value. A basic winch system consists of a constant torque storage drum, an overrunning clutch and line.

The aerodynamically-tethered balloon is the next logical step in hot air ballooning. In accomplishing this, improvements to the heat distribution network are needed to assure uniform temperature throughout the envelope. As a certain amount of air is constantly being driven into the envelope to support combustion, a venting system to balance the outflow with the inflow is essential while maintaining constant pressurization. Any natural leakage from the presently-designed balloons may be considered reasonable for balancing out needed inflow caused by combustion. As the high winds

Helium ball used in logging operations. Normally, it would be left flying on its tether from one day's shift to another.
(Raven Industries)

A 53,000 cubic foot logging balloon in its "bedded down" position. The balloon is brought down to this position for service, major maintenance or when not in use for a prolonged period. The heavy-lift balloon is for short haul of heavy tonnage material over difficult or rugged terrain.
(Raven Industries)

may cause heat losses, the aerodynamic balloon requires an insulated skin and a venting system.

The recent innovation of the Skyhook-logging balloon, developed by Goodyear Aerospace, Soderberg and Raven Industries, permits logging from inaccessible areas to roads or waterways, at lower levels, at minimum expense, and acceptable environmental conditions.

The Forest Research Institute of Sweden first investigated balloon for logging in 1956. In 1963, a Canadian, using a variation of the Swedish concept, demonstrated balloon logging in British Columbia, using two barrage balloon in tandem. In that same year, Goodyear Aerospace conducted the first flight of its "baby" Vee-Balloon for the Defense Department. The following January, the U.S. Forest Service contracted with Goodyear to investigate the economic and design aspect of balloon logging; the timber business being a $25 billion a year industry, with $3 billion being spent on direct harvesting of timber! The timber business works on a 100-year cycle; that is,

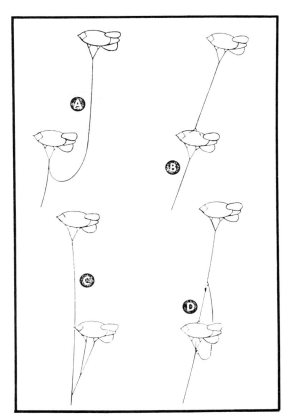

Sky Anchor— Tandem Aerostat Designs

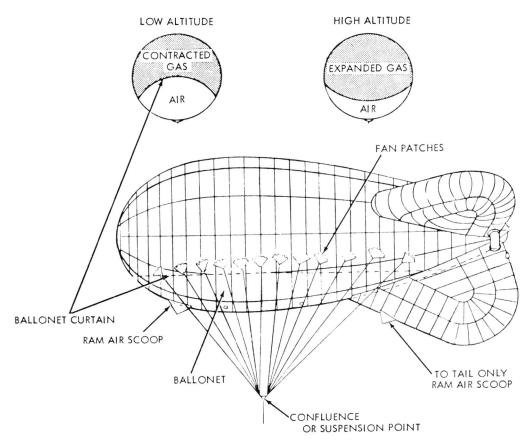

A tethered balloon design.

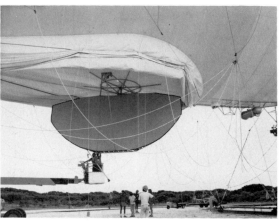

Tethered Aerostat Radar System (TARS), formerly called Seek Skyhook, being used as a platform to hoist a 1,000 lb. radar payload aloft which provides low-altitude surveillance at certain locations. The system is designed to hoist its payload to an altitude of 10,000–12,000 feet and maintain a stable platform for extended periods of time. The 250,000 cubic-foot aerostat is about 175 feet long, 60 feet across the hull and has a tip-to-tail dimension of around 80 feet.

Time aloft is only limited by the fuel onboard and weather. The system uses less than one gallon of fuel an hour and is stable in all but very severe weather. TARS out-performs any ground-based station by virtue of its performance at the higher altitude. (USAF Photo)

SMUGGLERS' SNITCH—The Mobile Aerostat Platform is part of a U.S. Coast Guard Marine Interdiction Surveillance Team plying the Caribbean to stop smugglers. The blimp flies at several thousand feet, tethered to the ship, providing a bird's-eye radar view of a 20,000 square mile area. On February 26, 1985, the coast guard leased another aerial balloon mounted radar system for law enforcement at sea, after successful performance of an earlier aerostat. The coast guard uses it in its drug interdiction program in combination with computers aboard ships, to which the aerostat is tethered. The system tracks target ships for drug smuggling. It is also used in enforcing fishing and other maritime laws, as well as for search and rescue operations. (TCOM Corp. Photo)

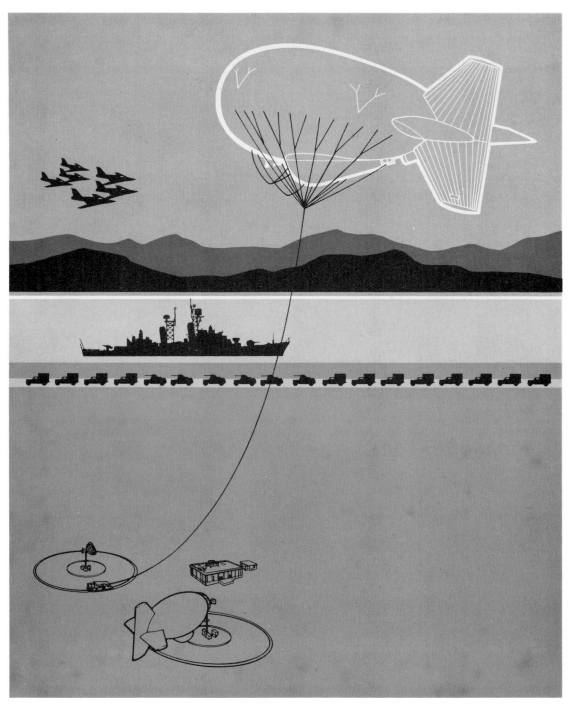

RCA aerostat system is an airborne surveillance radar and communication complex using a tethered-aerostat platform. The platform provides the USAF an accurate over-the-horizon radar coverage, using a lightweight S-band radar for early warning of any air, sea or land penetraton. Its airborne power generator provides for an on-station time of 5-plus days without refueling.
(RCA Service Co. Photo)

1% of the timber is harvested each year. Under the present logging techniques, only 45% of this timber was available. With balloon logging, an estimated 75% could be harvested, hauling logs above steep hillsides to the loading area.

Captive Vee-Balloons, among other types, favorably demonstrated logging timber techniques over extremely rough terrain. Using a huge 75,000-cubic-foot Vee-Balloon (built by Goodyear), tons of heavy logs were quickly moved over both distances and deep canyons from the logging site to their loading onto trucks.

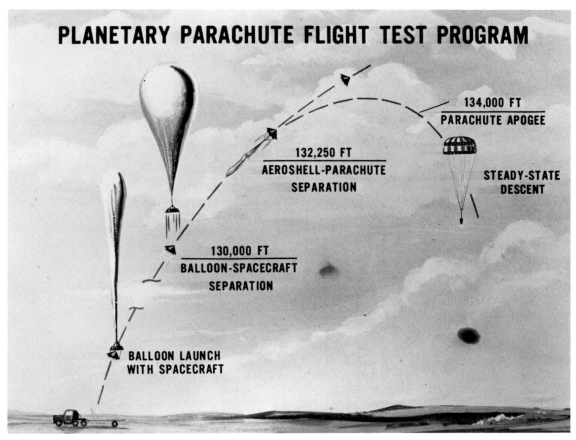

PLANETARY PARACHUTE FLIGHT TEST PROGRAM

134,000 FT
PARACHUTE APOGEE

STEADY-STATE
DESCENT

132,250 FT
AEROSHELL-PARACHUTE
SEPARATION

130,000 FT
BALLOON-SPACECRAFT
SEPARATION

BALLOON LAUNCH
WITH SPACECRAFT

Artist's concept of flight test unit from which parachutes are deployed in a series of experiments by NASA to check out new techniques for landing unmanned capsules on Mars. The unit will be carried to 140,000 feet by a huge Voyager balloon.

(NASA Photo)

(h) Viking Project

In 1972, NASA conducted a series of very high altitude flight tests over New Mexico in the process of developing a parachute system that would subsequently lower NASA's Viking Lander gently to the surface of Mars four years later.

In the initial subsonic tests, a zero-pressure helium-filled balloon carried the test spacecraft to a height of 92,000 feet. From this altitude, the spacecraft was allowed to free-fall into the desired subsonic speeds. In the final tests, the simulated Mars entry vehicle was carried to a height of 120,000 feet by a 34.6-million-cubic-foot balloon. The spacecraft was then released from the balloon and rocketed, at high velocity to an altitude of 147,000 feet. The entire assembly at the time of the launch was 890 feet tall. The test spacecraft and the ballast containers for the balloon system were carried beneath the recovery parachute on the metal framework known as a "load bar." Beneath the main balloon a cluster of three 100-foot parachutes were provided to lower the test craft

to the ground should the test have to be aborted.

Successful completion of the test qualified the Viking Parachute system for the Mars mission. The goal was to land two instrumented, unmanned spacecraft on the surface of Mars to search for evidence of past, present or potential future life on Mars.

The balloon system used in these tests was manufactured by the G.T. Schjeldahl Corporation. The Air Force Cambridge Research Laboratory handled the launching effort.

(i) Mars Voyager

Inflatable spacecraft have offered great potential for exploring planets such as Mars and Venus. In this role, the balloon concept has been considered for such uses as a "support vehicle" carrying measuring equipment; as a "conveyor" for moving objects from one point to another; and as a sensor for tracking and recording motions. No simpler and more economical method of transportation can be imagined.

The 815-foot tall Voyager aerostat was born from such considerations. This aerostat was a two-part, zero-pressure, interconnected system, with a main balloon surmounted by a small launch balloon. In size it stands between the Washington Monument's 555 feet and the 1,250 feet of the Empire State Building.

The Voyager design enabled its main balloon to remain reefed in a protective sleeve during the ground inflation and launch procedures. Its small upper balloon was first inflated and launched, then the main balloon zipped free. As the entire system ascended, gas from the small, upper balloon increased in volume and expanded into the main balloon.

Voyager balloon technology represented an advance in materials construction and balloon design. The bag itself was made from laminated Mylar and Dacron fibers of extremely lightweight 1 mil. (0.0035) thickness. This combination material was fabricated on a special loom called a Flying Thread Loom. The loom tailors the lamination of the material to match the payload and altitude requirements of any particular flight. The manner in which the loom continuously varies the angle of the weave and the density of the thread patterns achieves the maximum strength at those points where the greatest stress occurs on the balloon's surface. This loom-made material produced a tensile strength thirty times that of the polyethylene traditionally used for high altitude balloon flights. It offered not only a high strength-to-weight ratio, but also great tear resistance.

To simulate the velocity and dynamic

Crewmen prepare NASA's experimental planetary entry parachute payload for testing. These experiments are simulating conditions encountered by similar vehicles entering the thin planetary atmosphere of Mars. (NASA Photo)

pressure of the Mars entry body, the 15-foot test vehicle was checked out by the Voyager tandem balloon at around 130,000 feet. At that altitude, the payload was released from the balloon at a flight axis pointed slightly upward. Then, twelve small rocket motors accelerated the test vehicle to Mach 1.2 in level flight. This velocity simulated closely the maximum anticipated speed for the capsule at the time it entered the Martian atmosphere.

The Voyager balloon was developed by the Schjeldahl Corporation for the Air Force Research Laboratories with Martin-Marietta Corporation building the payload and flight unit, and integrating the parachute package into the flight unit.

(j) Venus Project

NASA also developed plans to explore the planet Venus using the balloon. While never developed beyond the planning stage, the general concept was to build a series of "floaters" which would be set adrift in the Venusian atmosphere. These floating stations were to gather scientific data from the lower atmosphere and from the surface of the planet. Once gathered, the information was to be relayed back to earth via a transmitting satellite orbiting the subject planet.

The type of information gleaned by such balloon probes was to include such things as: the horizontal location of the floating probe; the altitude, the atmospheric pressure, temperature, density, composition and wind velocity. Other meteorological data collected would include such things as: electromagnetic fields, gravitation and radiation, measurements below the buoyant station dealing with surface radiation and its characteristics, the cloud top and height, and the composition of the cloud particles.

(k) Russian & French Projects

Picking up where the United States left off, France and the Soviet Union launched Venera 83, a project designed to place two balloons into the mysterious sulfuric-acid clouds circling the planet Venus; which perpetually obscures its surface. This was the first time France had a role in planetary exploration, so long the province of the United States and the Soviet Union. (The U.S. was invited to participate in this venture, but was already committed to the Pioneer program.)

Jaques Blamont, France's chief space scientist was the architect of this unique effort. He believed that the four U.S. probes of Venus made previously under the Pioneer program were weak in what they revealed about the dynamics of the Venusian sulfuric-acid clouds. Blamont's intent with the Venera project was to examine more carefully the updrafts, sidewinds and downdrafts that appeared to be churning the clouds.

France built the two 27-foot high balloons which carried the instruments to measure such data as the Venusian horizontal and vertical wind changes in the clouds. The Russians suplied the two rocket spacecraft that carried the balloons on their journey. The balloons were packed in metal spheres which dropped into the planet's atmosphere where they opened up and released their cargo over the Venusian nightside. The two spacecraft then took up planetary orbits, acting as relay stations to earth. France also supplied the 66 pounds of instruments for each balloon and furnished some of the 170 pounds of instruments that were aboard each of the orbiters. Among the instruments France made for the orbiter was an ultra-violet telescope to measure the chemical makeup of the Venusian stratosphere and the tops of the clouds.

The construction of the French balloons consisted of five separate layers of plastic, the innermost and outermost being made of Teflon in order to resist the corrosive effects of the acid clouds. The most difficult part of constructing the balloons, according to Blamont, was finding a glue which would bond the five layers together.

Once released into the atmosphere, the balloons began to inflate with helium at a height of about 37 miles. They then descended to the bottom of the cloud layer where they completed their inflation and from there rose back through the strata. This climb leveled off at an altitude of about 35 miles. The aerostats was then in the zone where Pioneer's instruments found a stratum consisting of sulfuric-acid and solid particles of free sulfur.

As the winds blow from the day side to the night side they carried the balloons away from the night side around to the day side of the planet. The balloons traveled from the night to the day side in about four days, which was none too soon, as the acid in the clouds could eat away the balloons' skin in six.

(l) 1976 National Research Council Report

In 1976 the National Research Council (NRC) published its report entitled, "The Uses of Balloons for Physics and Astronomy" which for the first time exhibited the varied range of uses to which balloons are being put by the scientists of this country. A broad segment of the scientific community assessed the balloon's limitations and potentials for scientific uses in physics and astronomy (atmospheric science was not included, that being the domain of the NCAR).

The NRC found that balloons have made, and continue to make, very significant contributions to science. That they continue to manifest important advantages over the alternatives of aircraft or spacecraft such as; short lead times; relatively low costs; greater availability of flight opportunities; and the potential of considerably increased effectiveness through low-cost technical improvement. In exploring the near-space environment, the NRC found that, while satellites provide broader area

A giant balloon stands ready to be launched from the Air Force Missile Development Center Holloman AFB, New Mexico, by a blue suit launch crew. Numerous balloons are launched each year in support of many government research programs. A 26 million cubic foot Voyager balloon, the largest launched to date was sent aloft from Holloman on July 18, 1966. (USAF Photo)

Preparation of an Air Force balloon system prior to launch. (USAF Photo)

coverage, they do not provide vertical profiles as accurate as those done by balloons. And another finding of the report was that the balloon has been an important vehicle for the development of spacecraft and space flight instrumentation; one example being the Skylab coronagraph which represented the final, improved design stemming from earlier balloon-borne models.

The report established that much unique work has been accomplished through the use of balloon-borne research. Some of these accomplishments being:

- Far-infrared astronomy has allowed a balloon-borne telescope to map the intense, infrared emmissions from the center of the galaxy.
- Discoveries of certain aspects of energetic X-rays and of gamma rays.
- Balloons have carried optical telescopes to altitudes where atmospheric viewing is far superior to that obtainable on the ground.
- Collection of cosmic dust particles which can only be accomplished in the atmosphere, because in space these particles move much too fast to be stopped by satellite collectors.

- Maps of the magnetospheric electric fields have been made by simultaneous flights of balloons launched from widely separated locations around the globe.
- Balloon-borne instruments have measured the trace constituents in the stratosphere revealing, for example, the emmission of nitrogen oxides from SST aircraft may have depleted the stratospheric ozone balance; and that man-made propellants from aerosol spray cans reaching the stratosphere are catalytically destroying the ozone.

The NRC concluded that scientific use of balloons will increase in relation to improvements in ballooning and especially capabilities allowing for the launching of balloons from sites in addition to the present major facilities around the world.

(m) Some Major Accomplishments of the '70s

The next generation of trans-Atlantic flights will be using a ballastless, or "Sky Anchor" balloon system which comprises two balloons in tandem. One is a standard

Largest electronic cosmic ray detector ever to be launched in a high altitude balloon flight was built by Washington University students. The information collected and analyzed should reveal important new data about the little understood cosmic rays.
(Schjeldahl Photo)

68

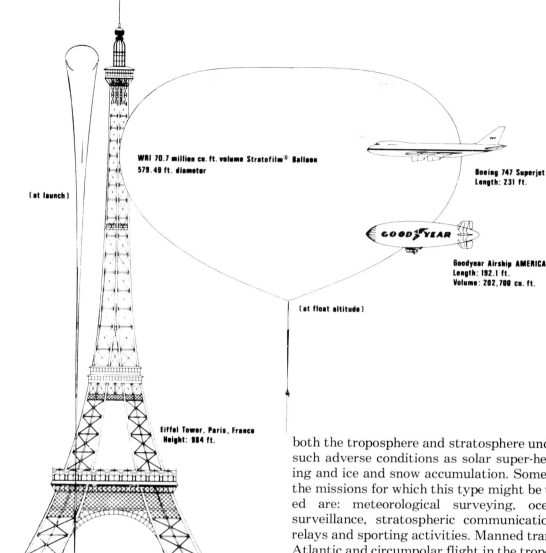

WRI 70.7 million cu. ft. volume Stratofilm® Balloon
579.49 ft. diameter

Boeing 747 Superjet
Length: 231 ft.

GOOD YEAR

Goodyear Airship AMERICA
Length: 192.1 ft.
Volume: 202,700 cu. ft.

(at launch)

(at float altitude)

Eiffel Tower, Paris, France
Height: 984 ft.

(Winzen International Drawing)

zero-pressure, polyethylene balloon providing the load-carrying capability and the other is a super-pressure, polyester sphere suspended 60 meters below, supplying the ballasting effect. Sky Anchor is being developed for long-duration, globe-circling flights as well as trans-Altantic operations.

Another compelling design related to long distance flight is the concept advanced by R.M. Dunlap of the U.S. Navy's Underwater Systems Center. Referred to as the "compound aerostat," this design uses a primary envelope filled with a lifting mixture of helium and methanol and a secondary envelope located within the first, filled with ammonia. The advantages of this peculiar configuration provide for long-duration flight in both the troposphere and stratosphere under such adverse conditions as solar super-heating and ice and snow accumulation. Some of the missions for which this type might be used are: meteorological surveying, ocean surveillance, stratospheric communications relays and sporting activities. Manned trans-Atlantic and circumpolar flight in the troposphere appears possible with this system. It also competes for exploration of atmospheres on other planets.

Due to the ever-increasing concern in recent years with the potential disruption of the apparently fragile chemical balance of the atmosphere either from natural or human causes, the U.S. Government launched Project LACATE (Lower Atmospheric Composition and Temperature Experiment) in 1974. This project, launched from White Sands, New Mexico, used a 45-million-cubic-foot balloon to carry a new, ten-channel, horizon-scanning radiometer to maximum altitude in order to obtrain data on such things as; temperature, ozone, water vapor, nitrogen dioxide, nitric acid, methane and flourocarbons. This device, once thoroughly tested, is destined for satellite flight.

Pioneering scientific achievement took place on August 8, 1975 when the first trans-

Atlantic balloon flight, launched from Trapani, Sicily, terminated near Lexington, Kentucky. Two other trans-Atlantic flights were launched in the summer of 1976, and while each of these flights carried different scientific experiments, all were alike in the route that they followed. Leaving Trapani, they reached float-altitude over the Mediterranean, overflew Spain and Portugal, then continued across the Atlantic to the United States.

The main features of this balloon system were an automatic ballasting system,

able; one was the cleanliness of the gas burst, and the other was the extremely distinct shock wave especially in high overpressure regions.

One of the 42 balloons flown by NASA in 1974 was the largest ever launched to that time. If laid out on the ground, it would have covered ten football fields, or 15 acres. When fully inflated the balloon had a volume of 50.3 million cubic feet. The plastic sheeting used in the balloon was so thin that the whole balloon weighed 2,956 pounds. The instrument package launched on this

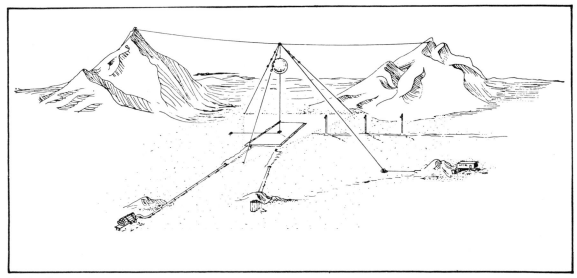

GEST (Gas Explosion Simulation Technique) program developed for the Defense Nuclear Agency by Schjeldahl. It tested nuclear explosions using detonable gas balloons. *(Schjedahl Photo)*

UFH/VHF telecommand system, an airborne and ground data system, an Omega navigation system and a 100-foot flat canopy parachute with which to recover the payload.

Something different in balloon-borne experiments was revealed by the U.S. Air Force in its results of the GEST (Gas Explosion Simulation Technique) Program conducted during the period 1973-74. This series of projects were performed for the Defense Nuclear Agency by the Schjeldahl Corporation; the manufacturer of the balloons used in the tests. These projects simulated nuclear explosions using detonatable gas balloons of varying magnitudes, from a yield of ten to thirty pounds up to a yield of 20 tons of high explosive. The reason balloons were used had to do with the need to study the entrainment of oxygen into the fireball of a low-altitude, nuclear explosion. Photographic and pressure measurements documented the movement of an explosive plasma and its surrounding medium.

Several factors made these tests desir-

aerostat measured the ratio of cosmic ray electrons to positrons.

A new and encouraging discovery occurred in August 1975, two years after a balloon-borne, cosmic-ray detection experiment was back to earth from 130,000 feet over Sioux City, Iowa. The telltale track, made through a sandwich of three dozen sheets of plastic, nuclear emulsion and photographic film, looked unfamiliar to the cosmic ray researchers. Two years later, scientists from the Universities of California and Houston finally offered an explanation. The unexpected particle was described as almost surely that of a magnetic monopole, the long sought basic unit of magnetism.

The new discovery, if eventually confirmed, will fill a gap in current scientific theory and modify present-day thinking about the basic building block of matter. Eventually, it might even have significant, practical application in research, medicine and the generation of energy.

The proof of the existence of the magnetic monopole would solve a mystery that had baffled scientists for more than a century, when Scottish physicist James C. Maxwell worked out the equation in 1865, describing in detail the symmetrical relationship between electricity and magnetism. In the past, physicists have searched for the monopole from the ocean floor minerals to meteorites and moon rocks, without success.

The possibility of monopole discovery, originally brought to light by the balloon, means that some of the laws of quantum electrodynamics, on which electronics and laser technology are based, will have to be revised to account for the new particle.

From 1971, tests and follow-up work with the Carrier Balloon System (CBS) resulted in a final report during August 1976. The CBS, a combination of seemingly unrelated elements: high altitude, super-pressure balloon; Omega retransmission dropsondes; and a Nimbus-6 position location system; when combined with a computer for data processing, proved a practical approach to systems building which might supplement remote satellite-sensing systems and conventional surface weather stations.

The latest test of CBS was conducted in the Fall of 1975 when 12 flights were launched from French Guiana with satisfactory results, except for the unexpected shorter-than-average balloon lifetime of 35 days. This appeared to be the result of a more severe infrared environment than was anticipated. The results from this test formed a reference for future design of improved reliability and performance of tropical data collection systems.

Another, in a continuing series of scientific balloons, was flown from New Zealand in January 1978 which was to become the forerunner to the electric-powered aerostat. The 30-foot diameter balloon was a part of the LAMB flights used to gather global atmospheric measurements and still maintain itself at a fixed latitude. The material used in a LAMB balloon would extend its lifetime as much as 10 years. The LAMB series was intended to be eventually outfitted with solar cells and a driving motor and propeller. If the balloon was to drift in latitude during the darkness, the solar-powered motor would chug away to return the 80-foot diameter aerostat to the desired latitude it was at during daylight hours. The LAMB

flights would allow tropical and southern hemisphere flights to be launched from the United States.

In 1978, the National Center for Atmospheric Research was ready to launch a long-lived, high-altitude balloon which was electric powered and able to maintain itself at a fixed altitude. Called LAMA (Long-lived Atmospheric Monitoring Balloon), it was outfitted with solar cells and a 100-watt motor driving a propeller to attain a cruise altitude of 66,000 feet. Unlike the Navy's HASPA, it was designed particularly for station-keeping in latitude.

Should the vehicle drift in latitude during darkness, the solar-powered 100-watt motor would return it to the designated latitude during daylight hours. The LAMA balloon was tracked by two NASA's satellites, telemetering data on the status and health of the balloon via the satellite or directly on high-frequency radio. The 30-foot diameter balloon, developed by Schjeldahl, used a new type of material that's expected to provide a 10-year lifetime to the balloon. This would be five times the longest lifetime ever achieved by a scientific balloon.

High altitude, powered balloons have been making good progress, but more work needs to be done in propeller design, drag-coefficient measurements and obtaining more accurate data on the dynamic stresses in the structure and their distribution over the balloon's surface.

The development of the instrumentation for space deployed systems was being performed in the '70s for the 1980's, through the BUSS (Balloon-borne Ultraviolet Stellar Spectrometer) system. The BUSS instrument payload has been flown aloft on numerous occasions and its performance successfully checked out as an ultraviolet radiation detector while at the same time it was also able to gather valuable astronomical data.

In 1979, the Air Force Geophysics Laboratory's Aerospace Instrumentation Division conducted a symposium at Portsmouth, New Hampshire, to determine the status and progress of balloon technology. A summary of these presentations follows:

1. A mobile LORAN (Long-Range Navigation) navigation system, designed by Arthur O. Korn of the Air Force Geophysical Laboratory, could provide an emergency replacement for the standard 400-foot

LORAN tower if it becomes inoperative or destroyed by severe weather or by enemy action. The balloon-borne antenna replacement would be a 45,000-cubic-foot, aerodynamically-shaped balloon to be tethered at 1,000 feet and lifting a 500-foot antenna with a tri-tether system. The tri-tethers serve additionally as top loaders for the antenna. The tethered balloon antenna system was successfully tested at Anniston, Alabama, in a series starting in 1978.

2. The Centre National D'Etudes Spatiales (CNES), Toulouse, France, updated the results of CNES balloon research and development program:

    a. For the scientific community, the open stratospheric balloon constitutes a platform with few constraints regarding technical planning, low costs and ease of access. It is possible to undertake experiments of a spatial nature having many diverse domains within a broad range of altitudes and without the need to use satellites. This is certainly true in the study of the dynamics, physics and photochemistry of the atmosphere. The long-duration balloon can be used independently or packed with remote sensing equipment.

Flotillas of pressurized, spherical balloons, several meters in diameter and fabricated with polyester film, has proved a fragile material with conflicting qualities, thus, CNES have been exploring the uses of composites in the superpressured, pumpkin-shaped balloon. Each of these elements possessed its own function: mechanical strength—Kevlar grid; gas barrier—thin polyester film; external protection—a flexible coating of, say, polyethylene.

    b. The traditional pressurized balloon of the quasi-spherical shape, used for hanging the gondola at the lower pole, has been the type of vehicle developed by CNES for the Franco-Soviet balloon project, in the exploration of Venus. The material contents of the nine-meter balloon included Kevlar fabric, aluminized polyester and another coating to

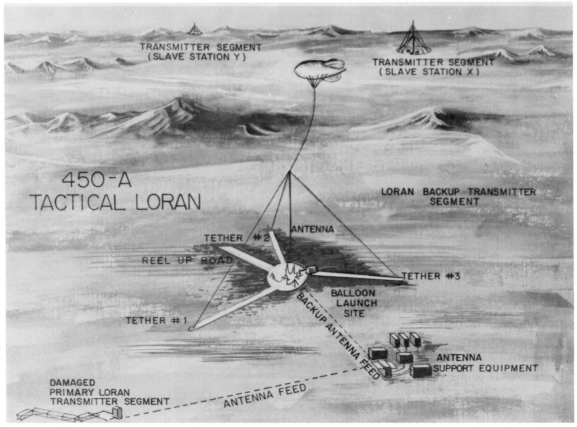

(USAF ESD/PAM Photo)

protect the envelope from aerosols of concentrated sulfuric-acid present in the Venusian clouds.

3. Heavy-Lift Balloon technology has been under scrutiny by NASA scientists W. Cuddihy and A. McHatton, together with Dr. R. Golden of New Mexico University since 1969. Launch operations and balloon manufacturing were also carefully examined. Their conclusion was that the heavy-lift launch techniques were marginal with the existing system. Between 1972 and 1977, 402 out of 468 flights were successful, an 86% success rate. Also, there was a high probability that some change in the balloon manufacturing or launch techniques had negatively shifted the margin for success since early 1977.

Two possible reasons for the heavy-lift balloon failures were explained to be due to damage or inherent defects of the balloon at inflation and release; and to leakage or bursting during ascent. Advance research is continuing to improve the technology in this area.

4. The National Scientific Balloon Facility (NSBF) at Palestine, Texas, operated by the University Corporation for Atmospheric Research under the sponsorship of the National Science Foundation, has been examining the tandem zero-pressure balloon system called the Sky Anchor. Its mission is to sustain a 500-pound payload at 130,000 feet for 100 days. Scientific research balloons, since the development of large plastic balloon of the early 1950's, have become the "poor man's" satellite platform. In these terms, Dr. I. Steve Smith, Jr., of the NSBF, presented an interesting report on the development of the Sky Anchor balloon system.

The zero-pressure balloon, fabricated from polyethylene materials, had offered a good load-carrying capability but due to the ballasting requirements has had a limited flight duration of hours or months, thus compelling the development of globe-circling balloons.

On the other hand, the large, unreinforced super-pressure balloons, while they are very stable, have lower payload-carrying capabilities and limited safety factors for surviving after an extended period of time. Consequently, the development of the zero- and super-pressure, Sky Anchor aerostat.

There are two basic ways of extending the float duration of a balloon. One, to use the natural-shape, unpressurized balloon, having a flight duration of between 5 to 8 days, and making use of its heavy-lift capability to support the heavy ballast load. The other is to fly a pressurized balloon, capable of withstanding high skin stress caused by overpressurization from the warm, daytime gas temperatures. This design has a very good altitude stability, as long as enough overpressure is maintained in the balloon to prevent it from going slack at night.

As a result of the success achieved by the National Center for Atmospheric Research's (NCAR) GHOST program, NSBF scaled up the smaller, unreinforced polyester super-pressure spheres with reasonably good results in establishing design parameters on which larger balloons could be built.

In addition, with the progress of the Boomerang balloon test flights, it was evident that unreinforced polyester film could not be fabricated into a single-cell, super-pressure spherical balloon, so as to achieve NCAR's long-duration program goals and still have a high degree of reliability. Naturally, a different approach was necessary.

It was then, in 1975, that the NSBF started to examine the potential of a hybrid zero-pressure/super-pressure balloon system

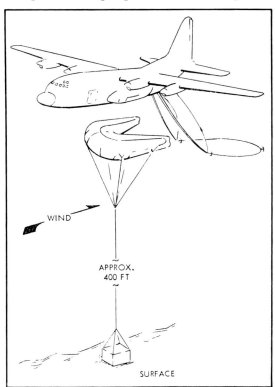

Goodyear Boomerang balloon, heavy load, Surface-to-Air Recovery System. *(Goodyear Drawing)*

73

Boomerang orbit.   *(NASA Photo)*

Scene during inflation of 46.1 million cubic feet balloon in Australia for the study of x-ray sources from space by MIT scientists.   *(Photo Dr. Walter Lewin)*

View of sophisticated 2000 pound payload of MIT x-ray experiment before launch in Australia, April 1972.
(Photo Dr. Walter Lewin)

Moment of launch of MIT x-ray experiment in Australia. The flight carried the 1-ton payload to an altitude of 45 km for a duration of 27 hours.
(Photo Dr. Walter Lewin)

which would require no diurnal ballasting. In order to counter the effects of sunset and subsequent loss of gas from the zero-pressure balloon, various air ballast systems have been looked at over the years, some requiring various type motors, blowers, winches, ducts and high-pressure containers.

The credit for the Sky Anchor concept goes to NCAR and its eminent Program Director V.E. Lally, when, in 1963 a Sky Anchor flight launched from the NCAR grounds at Boulder, Colorado, flew for two days at the designed altitudes through two sunsets, a considerable achievement for an unballasted, zero-pressure balloon.

This attainment was followed by the Air Force Cambridge Research Laboratories using the Sky Anchor system in 1968. The main balloon was constructed of polyethylene and the super-pressure ballast balloon was made from tri-laminate Mylar.

The latest Sky Anchor system has been a super-pressure balloon carried aloft by a zero-pressure main balloon. As the main balloon reaches its operational altitude, the super-pressure balloon fills up and becomes pressurized. While the "super-pressure" vehicle floats upward, it loses more and more

lift. As sunset comes on, the entire system descends to a new equilibrium where the increase in lift of the super-pressure aerostat about equals the effect of the sunset on the main balloon. At sunrise, the main balloon expands and the system rises again. In doing so, the super-pressure balloon loses the lift it gained at sunset, with the system stabilizing at the same altitude as the preceding day.

In a succeeding year, 1977, the Sky Anchor II was tested at Palestine, Texas, achieving a float altitude of 94,400 feet for 47 hours and through two nights without ballasting. The payload package was recovered in excellent condition after being successfully flown and terminated.

Following in this series was Sky Anchor VII which was tested in May, 1978, carrying instruments for altitude monitoring, a differential pressure gauge, air temperature monitoring, down radiometer, a video camera and two super 8mm surveillance cameras. The Sky Anchor flight leveled off around 112,000 feet but soon after was terminated because of liquid ballast failure. To correct this problem, no liquid pressurization ballast was to be carried on future

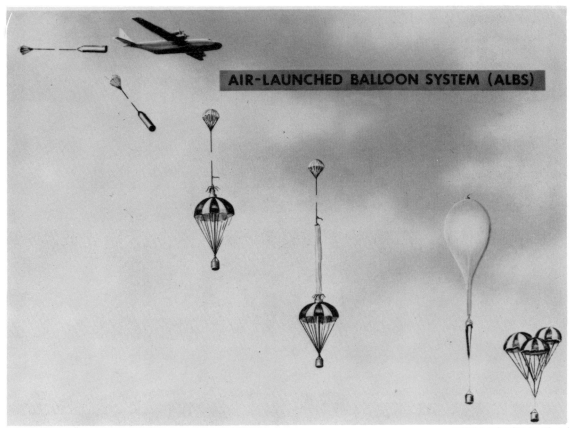

AIR-LAUNCHED BALLOON SYSTEM (ALBS)

(USAF ESD/PAM Photo)

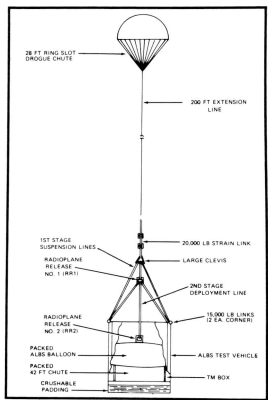

ALBS balloon package. (USAF ESD/PAM Photo)

flights. With the present state-of-the-art, super-pressures can lift a 2,000-pound payload to 120,000 feet.

5. The Air Launched Balloon System (ALBS), reported by Andrew S. Carten, Jr., of the Air Force Geophysics Laboratory, is a quick-reaction, lighter-than-air, tactical communications relay platform positioned at high altitudes; or referred to in military terms as a satellite Airborne Communications Relay System for Tactical Air Forces.

The ALBS package is made up of a cryogenic helium unit, a packed 42-foot parachute, a packed air-launch balloon and an electronic control package. The ALBS package is extracted from an airborne C-130 military aircraft at 25,000 feet, followed by a mid-air inflation of the polyethylene balloon by an attached helium storage unit. A launch was performed in a three-stage operation. The first stage was the package being withdrawn from the aircraft and its transition to a vertical altitude. The second stage covered the deployment of the main chute, 200 feet beneath the drag chute. The third stage covered the extraction of the balloon from its container on top of the opened main chute and the inflation to full extension of the balloon. After completing the three steps, the parachute array became ready to descend earthward. The inflated balloon

was able to carry a 200-pound communications relay to its assigned altitude of 70,000 feet, while the parachute subsystem floated the inflation hardware to the ground.

6. Charles F. Sindt of the U.S. National Bureau of Standards, Boulder, Colorado, illustrated the airborne technique for inflating a balloon with helium. The helium, used for inflation, is stored in a liquid state and later converted to gas by use of a hotbed heater exchanger. This self-contained system is activated by a single electrical signal.

The air-launch balloon system, the balloon, its payload and inflation equipment, is extracted from a flying aircraft by a small parachute. The system descends briefly before a larger parachute is deployed, after which the small parachute extracts the balloon from a bag secured to the canopy of the large parachute and extends it vertically. The balloon is then ready to be inflated with helium. Mid-air inflation takes about five minutes. The system descends, in the process, to about 12,000 feet. On completion of the inflation, the inflation unit separate from the rest of the system, which descends to the ground on a three-parachute cluster. The filled balloon ascends then to the

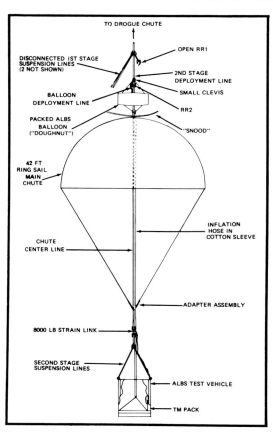

Parachute Test System, ALBS (air launched balloon system). (USAF ESD/PAM Photo)

desired altitude, carrying the payload and the large parachute which is later employed to recover the payload.

7. Dr. J. Craig Erickson of New Mexico State University evaluated the facilities in the flight support of scientific balloons. The two major balloon launch facilities in the United States are located at the Air Force's Holloman Air Force Base and the National Scientific Balloon Facility at Palestine, Texas.

Scientists depend on these facilities for data collection, telemetry, recording, display, and command and control. Economy is attained through commonality and standardization of support hardware and software. Collected data are recorded on an analog and digital magnetic tape for analysis at the ground stations.

8. Julian P.P. Nott of the Hot Air Balloon Company, Ltd., London, focused on the scientific, multidisciplinary approach. By way of introduction, Mr. Nott pointed out that most sport balloonists, the end users of the nexus of many sciences, are woefully ignorant of the activities of the scientific community. The scientific range being from basic physics and chemistry through materials science, combustion, aerodynamics and static, communications and navigation, aviation medicine and life-support systems and a significant amount of meteorology.

In 1972, Julian Nott, with two other balloonists, crossed the Sahara Desert in a hot air balloon. This was the first successful use of mathematical modeling in hot air ballooning, and not the last. Nott teamed up again in 1973 to fly over the Alps in a conventional gas balloon to Italy. Then again in 1974, their goal was an altitude record, using for the first time a 95-pound hot air balloon pressure cabin made of fiberglass and windows of Mylar. One of the windows was large enough to allow for a rapid parachute escape. Fuel was carried in racks on the outside and the cabin had 6-inch sponge rubber shoes for landing. The flight was routine, reaching 46,000 feet. Mathematical modeling was employed to estimate fuel consumption and a handling model to aid in flying the balloon because of its large volume.

9. An interesting concept for the AT-MOSAT super-pressure balloon system was presented in 1978 by the Jet Propulsion Laboratory as part of a mission to explore Mars. The "Roving Ball Planetary Explorer" would be an instrument-laden, rein-forced-fabric ball capable of inflating and deflating automatically, or by remote command from Earth. Driven by the high winds known to prevail on Mars' surface, any number of these balloons or bouncing balls could roam the surface almost at random, as they conduct scientific experiments and measurements over vast areas.

The "bouncing ball" can be low-cost, long-life and could have an extended traverse of the Martian terrain. It would carry a 44- to 66-pound payload over an area 60 to 120 miles and be strong enough to survive the Martian atmosphere.

A typical Mars mission, using the giant balls, could deploy different sized balls, ranging from 10 to 33 feet in diameter. Each one could be equipped with command inflation and deflation, an adjustable center of gravity, pressurization by a blower using Mars' carbon dioxide and an instrument payload suspended within each ball.

With the balls fully inflated, they could be blown across the surface by the Martian winds, much like a tumbleweed. Partially inflated, with the center of gravity lowered close to the flattened "foot" that has been formed, the ball can be fixed in position. If powered, the ball would require only 10 watts to travel 2 miles per hour.

By manipulating the pressure and center of gravity within each ball, its motion could be started and stopped under any prevailing wind condition. By sensing wind conditions and force, the ball could be maneuvered over the Martian surface. Adjustment to the pressure and center of gravity gives the ball the ability to surmount obstacles to a height equal to around one-third the diameter of the ball.

The two Viking landers that gathered information on the Martian surface, showed the terrain to be generally rugged and strewn with large boulders. There is a possibility of an inflatable ball becoming entrapped by a very large obstacle. Such a location would be of special scientific interest, as a large accumulation of wind-blown Martian materials could also be trapped there.

The ATMOSAT-manned super-pressure balloon can remain stable in a parcel of air without agitating the air chemistry in any way. Such a system permits precise determination of air trajectories over many miles of land and water. The employment of

Stratospheric research balloons like these are used to measure cosmic rays from distant galaxies, man-made contaminants in the upper atmosphere and a host of other scientific experiments.   *(NCAR/NSF Photo)*

trained observers aboard can facilitate the collection of atmospheric data to include ozone, NO_x, SO_2, temperature gradients, turbulence, among others.

The balloon system is a low-cost, recoverable vehicle that neither contaminates the air by any propellant fumes, nor agitates it by propeller wash. It does gather accurate data in a new dimension of today's air pollution control effort. The proposed Roving Ball Planetary Explorer does offer a new function for the ATMOSAT system.

IV

A LOOK AT THE
'80s & BEYOND

The potential of expandable space structures promises much: they are lightweight and can be folded into high-density packages requiring relatively little lift to be placed in orbit. When in space they can be rapidly inflated and by injecting quicksetting foam between inner and outer layers, can be made rigid; can be fabricated from plastic and fiber to tolerances as strong as steel; and they can be designed to adopt almost any shape and to serve many different functions. They could function to reflect electronic signals, gather solar energy, provide safe shelter or become orbital stations; they might serve as simple storage facilities for gases or fuels or become complex platforms for powerful telescopes; the list is really limited only by one's resourcefulness.

The United States space program is dedicated to increasing the knowledge of the universe through aeronautical and space technology. From our decade-long odyssey to reach the Moon, a technical foundation has been created that will provide the base from which shall rise a virtually new age of exploration. Already the shuttle effort has considerably reduced operating costs while increasing launch capability. We can now enter and exit space with much greater ease.

The commercialization of space are concepts born form our present abilities. The goods and services produced in space *will* have a major economic benefit here on earth. The boon of manufacturing in a weightless environment is one with many specific applications, for example, electric power generation; the development of new processes for the creation of new materials, chemicals and medicines, a newly founded communications

industry; a more comprehensive weather services and earth resource management; all will find reality through the exploration of space. Ultimately we will industrialize the Moon and more.

By 1984, the U.S. Air Force was operating a tethered aerostat antenna as an alternate to the operation of VLF (very low frequency) transmitting facilities, in the event of emergencies and in maintaining secured communications. The ground-based VLF facility lacked survivability in combat or against terrorism. Thus, the rapidly deployable aerostat became the likely candidate for reestablishing communications.

Then, there is the Westinghouse Tethered Communications, a 25,000-cubic-foot STARS (Small Transportable Aerostat Relocatable System) balloon which operates at a 3,000-foot altitude and using a special Kevlar tether line as an antenna. Westinghouse has packaged its services, from design to operations, of its aerostat system. The STARS design has been used in oil surveillance, overseas communications, cold-weather survival testing by the U.S. Air Force, and working with the U.S. Custom Service, to interdict drug traffic in the Caribbean area with electronically-equipped aerostats.

A remote-controlled, airborne laboratory, perched in the stratosphere at 133,000 feet, had its day in scientific accomplishments. It was September 15, 1982, over the NSBF near Palestine, Texas, where scientist James Anderson launched his 700-foot tall balloon, lifting a 1½-ton scientific test platform which included a special 130-pound chemistry lab attached to a motor-driven winch. Extending from the winch was a thin Kevlar cord extension of nearly 10 miles long. After the balloon rose some 25 miles, Anderson pulled the pin on the winching platform by remote control, thus deploying the tethered lab onto the Kevlar cordage. The winch setting on the platform reeled the lab downward nine and a half miles, then it was reeled back up like a yo-yo after it had conducted some uninterrupted testing of chemical composition of the unstable molecules in the ozone layer, ultraviolet radiation that causes skin cancer and of fluorocarbons, a manmade chemical used in aerosol cans, and its effects.

Years earlier, in 1976, James Anderson delivered to a Congressional Committee hearing some strong chemical evidence that fluorocarbons did indeed threaten the critical ozone layer. From his observations he described the relationship between the two, and for the future, a window to the significance of the ozone layer.

After completing the stratospheric lab work, the tethered lab was released from the balloon by remote control and it descended by parachute to a landing area 25 miles from the launch site. The instruments remained intact and became available for use on another mission.

The National Center for Atmospheric Research (NCAR) of the 80's has become a sophisticated, computerized center for university-based, scientific research of the atmosphere. NCAR is now sponsored by the National Science Foundation, the federal agency having primary interest in supporting basic research. NCAR is governed and operated by the University Corporation for Atmospheric Research whose 53 member universities comprise most of the universities in the United States with a doctoral program in the atmospheric sciences. Also being governed by the Corporation is the National Scientific Balloon Facilities (NSBF) located at Palestine, Texas, which is under contract with NASA. Many of the major scientific balloon flights are made from NSBF.

At the onset of the 1980's, high-altitude scientific ballooning had become a formidable and cost-effective means of scientific research in astronautics and aeronautics. Significant technological achievements were demonstrated by increased payload capacity, reliable communications, longer flight duration and increased reliability of flight

and payload recovery. Scientific accomplishments in the fields of atmospheric chemistry and physics, astronomy and astrophysics became commonplace because of the balloon. Also, astronautical endeavors of the balloon have brought forth new and fundamental knowledge of our galaxy, its composition and structure, and of the entire extragalactic universe.

In an October, 1982 report by the University Corporation for Atmospheric Research (UCAR), new advances were recommended toward extending flight durations, developing a capability to launch balloons regularly over a range of geographic latitudes, and achieving higher float altitudes, primarily for atmospheric chemistry and to a lesser degree, for astrophysical investigations.

On October 1, 1982, NSBF became an independent UCAR operation under the National Aeronautics and Space Administration (NASA) sponsorship. On April 1, 1984, NCAR was awarded a contract by NASA's Wallops Flight Facility to run the NSBF where there were some sixty to seventy scientific balloons being launched each year.

In prospective, there has been a concern about man's activities on the earth's surface affecting the chemical composition of the stratosphere and disturbing the ozone layer with it.

The injection of gases and dust into the stratosphere by natural processes, as with volcanic explosions, can also cause change in the ozone layer. Changes in the amount of ozone in the stratosphere can lead to adverse ecological effects while any change in the vertical distribution of ozone may lead to undesirable climatic change.

The United States and other countries have joined together in scientific research programs to conduct investigations in such areas as chemistry and physics of atmospheric ozone and its sensitivity to change.

An international team of scientists in 1981 successfully calibrated a number of sensitive instruments that were used to measure minute amounts of water vapor . . . a very important component in the stratosphere.

Representatives of the scientific groups participating in the tests were: The British National Physical Laboratory; Canada's Atmospheric Service; the National Oceanic and Atmospheric Administration (NOAA); the Naval Research Laboratory; the Univer-

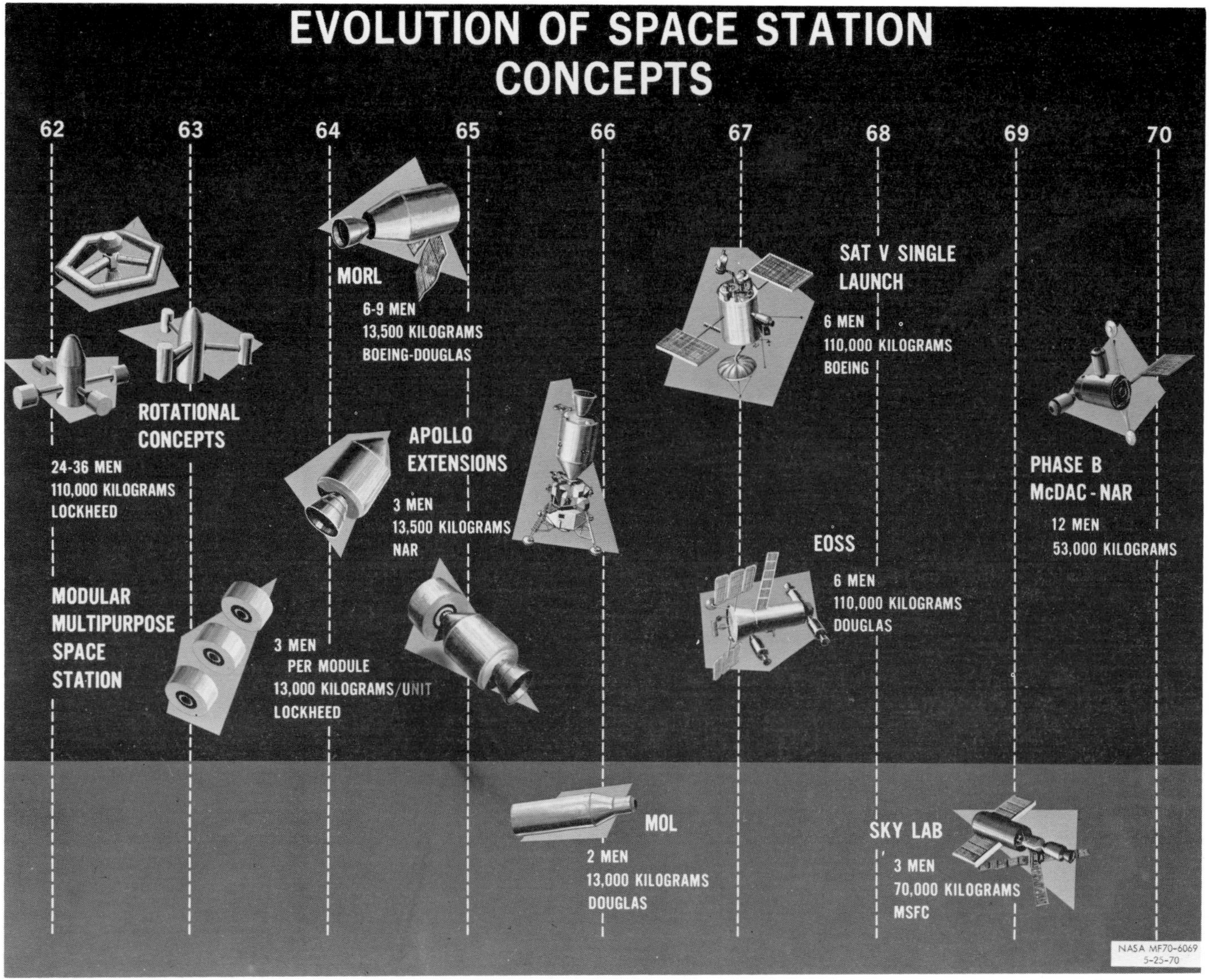

EVOLUTION OF SPACE STATION CONCEPTS

ROTATIONAL CONCEPTS
24-36 MEN
110,000 KILOGRAMS
LOCKHEED

MORL
6-9 MEN
13,500 KILOGRAMS
BOEING-DOUGLAS

MODULAR MULTIPURPOSE SPACE STATION
3 MEN PER MODULE
13,000 KILOGRAMS/UNIT
LOCKHEED

APOLLO EXTENSIONS
3 MEN
13,500 KILOGRAMS
NAR

SAT V SINGLE LAUNCH
6 MEN
110,000 KILOGRAMS
BOEING

EOSS
6 MEN
110,000 KILOGRAMS
DOUGLAS

PHASE B McDAC-NAR
12 MEN
53,000 KILOGRAMS

MOL
2 MEN
13,000 KILOGRAMS
DOUGLAS

SKY LAB
3 MEN
70,000 KILOGRAMS
MSFC

NASA MF70-6069
5-25-70

(NASA Photo)

Inflatable space station concepts were established early in NASA space activities.

81

sities of Minnesota and Denver; and the NCAR under the sponsorship of the National Science Foundation (NSF).

Helium-filled balloons, each the size of a football field, carried instruments weighing six to 2,000 pounds which simultaneously collected measurements of the water vapor. At these altitudes only trace amounts of water vapor are present. What little there is enters into a wide range of important chemical reactions and influences the behavior of infrared radiation, from sunlight, in the lower stratosphere.

Obtaining accurate measurements of water vapor in the stratosphere has been problematic. Many groups independently have taken measurements, but, the question is, whose technique is more accurate?

To resolve this key question, the FAA and NASA have sponsored a project to cross-check seven techniques for measuring water vapor in the stratosphere up to 138,000 feet altitude using zero-pressure polyethylene balloons.

NCAR prefers to use balloons. They are more versatile and can be sent up at any given point, covering a much broader horizontal parcel of air, and filling the altitude gap between conventional aircraft and the rocket. Unlike satellites, balloons are useful in taking exact vertical profile measurements at given points in the atmosphere.

NASA was interested in discovering how water vapor gets into the stratosphere and how much it varies in concentration with altitude and/or latitude. Water vapor profiles have differed greatly. Either the stratosphere's composition varies widely or there are substantial differences in the precision of the instruments.

FAA has been also supporting research into the problem of stratospheric ozone destruction and particularly into the effects of emissions from high-flying aircraft. Such aircraft emits oxides of nitrogen and water vapor.

Future intercomparisons of instruments measuring other constituents are a part of this on-going program, linking the present with the past.

Past measurements using airborne instruments have not been entirely well coordinated in terms of space and time. Also, there is the natural variability of the atmosphere, which is not well known, and which therefore makes it difficult to assess the accuracy of past measurements, or determine

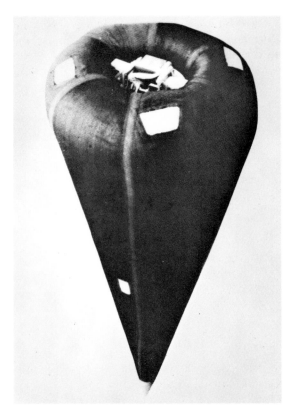

The IEO, an inflatable erectable decoy for Minuteman.
(L'Garde, Inc. Photo)

whether the differences in measurement were due to atmospheric variations, or inaccuracies in the instruments.

Available measurements were not sufficient and their accuracies insuffiently tested to provide a good verification of computer models. Designed to improve this situation, and provide greater use of the measurements, was the Balloon Intercomparison Campaign (BIC), which was developed to intercompare the results from separate instruments. BIC was divided into two flights, one in September 1982, the other in the Spring of 1983. Each flight consisted of the near simultaneous launch from Palestine, Texas, of four balloons carrying a total of 17 instruments from laboratories of 7 different countries. Data from the NOAA-7 satellite was also collected at the time of these flights.

The BIC assessed the accuracy of scientific instruments in current use; each making its chemical composition measurements of the stratosphere at the same time and in the same air mass. Consequently, any atmospheric variability was removed and any specific instrument suffering from excessive inaccuracy was detected. From these results, better measurement strategies were being designed.

In January 1983 a report by the Long Duration Balloon Flight Study Committee was published by NCAR with sponsorship from NASA and NSF, setting forth its plan to provide for the need of the long-duration flights, the flight-support system and the methods to support them.

The Committee concluded that the next major advancement in scientific ballooning will be an operational long-duration flight program, which would include circumglobal (Southern Hemisphere) flights lasting from weeks to months, as well as the transcontinental and transoceanic flights of extended duration.

Coincidentally, the tandem Sky Anchor system, which carried a 1200-pound payload and had a limited operational flight capability, expected to reach full capability within a few years. To accomplish this, however, technical advances were required in balloon vehicles and flight-support systems for long-duration flights; particularly in the area of global telecommunications and navigation systems, power systems, and the control of several simultaneous experiments circumnavigating the earth. The Committee recommended that a vigorous long-duration balloon program, open to other nations, be initiated directly.

One of NCAR's programs that has progressed well is the global Atmospheric Measurements Program (GAMP) in which new techniques have been designed to provide accurate soundings and measurements of the atmosphere. GAMP developed the Safesonde, a balloon-borne system to measure the winds occurring between the earth's surface and the lower stratosphere. This information was needed for the major mesoscale research program planned for the late 1980's that will include Stormscale.

Prototypes of the system, called Safesonde, have been tested out with the high-precision radars at Wallops Island, Virginia. Safesonde has no moving mechanical parts and can be produced at a fraction of the cost of tracking-antenna systems of radar and radio-direction finders.

GAMP launched ten Safesondes in September 1982 from Wallops Test Facility, at which time they exceeded all of the designed goals. Safesonde's ability to make fast response measurements of temperature and humidity as well as fine-scale wind structure will enable new insights into the mesoscale weather phenomena. This system will be-

come a new and essential tool for the national STORM program and other major mesoscale programs being planned for the next decade, requiring a network of high-resolution vertical sounding stations.

Another GAMP program dealt with floating weather stations. NCAR envisioned using a portable, easy-to-operate weather station that could be installed on commercial ships crossing the Pacific and Atlantic Oceans. The effort was called the Automated Shipboard Aerological Program (ASAP), and it was designed to launch weather balloons for upper-air soundings over the oceans. Meteorologists have a keen interest in receiving increased weather data from the oceans that spawn storms and affect the mainlands.

The weather balloon platform is fitted into a sea container where it is inflated, then lifted through a hatch for launching to an elevation of 90,000 feet. The signals sent by the balloon-borne instrument package are reports of the wind, pressure, temperature and humidity which are received by the ship and then processed by microcomputer for transmission by satellite to an NCAR receiving station at Boulder, Colorado. From there, the data are sent to weather services worldwide.

Another GAMP creation in 1983 was a balloon system to study the electrodynamics of the middle atmosphere (EMA). With the support of NASA and NSF, a consortium of universities have been engaged in measuring the atmosphere's electrical conductivity, magnetic field, pressure and temperature fluctuations, local ionization and lightning strikes. Some of the prototypes were flown in March from New Zealand, with six more EMA balloons launched during a six-month program beginning in November 1983.

Since World War Two there have been many notable technolgocial accomplishments emanating from scientific ballooning and its combination of instrument technology and balloon capability. At the same time, there is a continuing need to upgrade the technology and operational support demanded by increasing flight capabilities associated with payload launch and recovery operations.

In part, this has been due to limited flights and space availability on NASA's Shuttles and satellites. Scientific ballooning continues to be the economical and technical means for fulfilling upper atmospheric and space research. Major advances in science will continue unbroken, as long as industry, government, and the scientific community work in close harmony and support a national aerospace balloon program.

Most scientific balloons carry remote-controlled instruments, instead of human observers and pilots, to record the data on tape or film, or to radio information back to the ground. These balloon-borne instruments have been observing the far reaches of our galaxy, the Milky Way, and have been searching for evidence of "black holes" where the force of gravity is so powerful that not even light can escape. Balloons will continue to uncover new knowledge on the origin of the stars, examine low-level radiation, which has been considered a remnant of the fireball contributing to the birth of our expanding universe, and to be of benefit in our everyday lives.

New and advanced materials, data systems and balloon designs have recently been

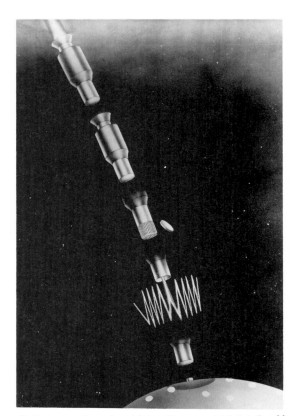

Early conception of a 12-foot-diameter folded inflatable satellite being ejected from its payload container and automatically inflated in space. The satellite, designed and fabricated at NASA's Langley Research Center, is covered with 3,600 small white-painted dots to provide better heat balance characteristics on its surface while in orbit.

(NASA Photo)

developed. Unequaled benefits to the scientific community are being accrued by the versatile balloon, particularly in the exploration of the near-space environment.

(a) Inflatable & Erectable Space Structures

Inflatable space structures, which originated with NASA in the 1950's, favored a marriage of the inflatables and the erectables to create space stations, satellites and other structure in which man can use and survive in the space environment. The inflatable components in the structure are packaged together and rocketed into space, inflated and rigidized. Its feasibility and efficiency were critically evaluated and accepted by NASA.

The practical, lightweight, packaged structure using the latest engineering designs has led to a relatively new technology, identified as inflatable, erectable, space structures, with varied shapes oriented to each mission. These expandable structures which include a collector system with high dimensional accuracy, that can be

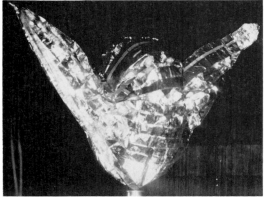

A 12-foot-diameter inflatable spherical satellite shown during ground inflation tests. The sphere is still attached to its container during initial stages of inflation in a vacuum chamber which simulated a space environment. After inflation the sphere detached from its container. A printed-wire cable (dark lines) connected solar cells with the satellite's storage battery pack and transmitter pack was used by ground tracking stations. *(NASA Photo)*

Lightweight inflatable satellites for use as radar targets and for measuring air density and other characteristics of space have been devised by scientists of NASA. Made of micro-thin plastic covered with aluminum foil, the satellites include 30" and 12' spheres, and a 12' corner reflector. These are intended for scientific experiments such as the measurement of air density and in studying reflection and scattering of radio and radar signals. The satellites are propelled into space in a deflated condition, ejected into orbit and automatically inflated by a nitrogen gas cartridge. Gas pressure is then allowed to escape to prevent the satellite from becoming propulsive in the event of puncture by a micrometeorite. Aluminum foil permits the satellites to maintain shape after pressure is released. *(NASA Photo)*

Technicians at the Langley Research Center of NASA begin preliminary folding of a 12-foot-diameter inflatable spherical satellite. The globe shown in the background was used in bonding together individual gores of the material during fabrication of the sphere, which was covered with 3,600 small white-painted dots to provide better heat balance characteristics on the surface while it is in orbit. *(NASA Photo)*

Fully inflated 12-foot diameter sphere as it will appear after ejection from payload container. *(NASA Photo)*

Two modelmakers fabricate a micro-thin 12-foot-diameter satellite similar to one in the foreground to be used in studying the characteristics of space. The satellite was designed to be carried aloft in a deflated condition, ejected into orbit by a rocket and automatically inflated. The satellites were constructed of a thin layer of Mylar plastic and covered on either side by aluminum foil. The three-layer laminated material was obtained commercially in rolls. In the construction of a 12-foot-diameter satellite, modelmakers cut the material into 40 gores which are laid over a molded shell. *(NASA Photo)*

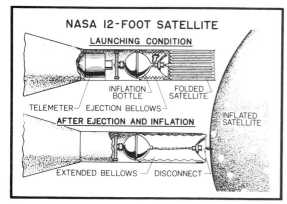

Two views of the payload (folded and inflated) to be launched from a Scout vehicle to determine the density of earth's atmosphere. *(NASA Photo)*

Explorer IX inflated satellite measures atmospheric density. The satellite was inflated after being launched into space and then injected into orbit. *(NASA Photo)*

folded up into small packages on the launch pad, propelled beyond the earth's atmosphere and rigidized in space. The ECHO series is a good example.

New materials, developed in combination with mineral fibers to become as strong as steel and non-combustible, have withstood the space environment for prolonged periods. Two manufacturers, Hughes Aircraft Company and Goodyear Aerospace Corporation, have produced rigid materials for many space applications.

All this was brought to the attention of the U.S. Congress on May 19, 1961. The Congressional Committee on Science and Astronautics conducted a hearing dealing with expandable space structures, after which the Committee submitted its final report to the Speaker of the House on August 15, 1961, for careful deliberation by the 87th Congress. The hearing came at a time when the nation was looking for ways to save precious time in the international race for space that was taking place, and reportedly felt that lightweight, expandable structures deserved the full attention of the space program.

The report revealed that very large shapes with low density carried through the atmosphere at high speeds or at high acceleration rates were then considered impractical. At the same time, inflatable structures were then capable of being folded into relatively small packages and accommodated in payload carriers on conventional launch vehicles. This was a definite advantage over rigid, preassembled devices of the same ultimate shape.

A NACA corner reflector satellite is large and bright enough not to require a radio beacon to help locate it. It can be used as a radar beacon for navigation, surveys, and could be traced into space. (NACA Photo)

Moreover, a typical foldable, expandable structure did not have the design complications or weighted penalties that a rigid structure would. The reliability of the ultimate structure, unfolded and inflated, was also much easier to design and test on the ground.

The Congressional Committee's report made known that the U.S. Air Force's interest in expandable structures may involve classified projects and would therefore not be appropriate for a public hearing. Mention was made by industry witnesses of two military interests; one involved solar collectors that could be rigidized in space, the other was an investigation of the military testing of numerous types of space stations.

The conclusions of the report made by the House Committee on Science and Astronautics were that:

- Work already done on all types of expandable and inflatable structures shows much promise and their applications are many; expandable structures have certain advantages over rigid structures; and with U.S. leadership and the economics of inflatables, a valuable contribution to our national goals in space can be made.
- NASA and DOD coordinate their work in expandable space struc-

Lightweight inflatable satellites designed to study air density, measurement of reflection and scattering of radar and radio signals. (NASA Photo)

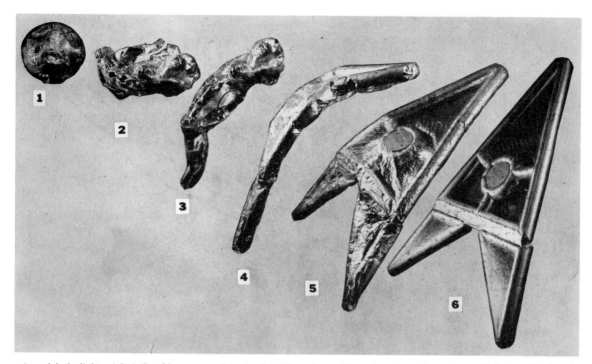

A model of a lightweight inflatable space craft in simulated launch condition, showing various stages of inflation. A full scale version of the venicle could be folded into a small container and kept until rocketed into space. It could be used for a ferry, crew quarters, or interplanetary spaceship. *(NASA Photo)*

tures and not overlook any potentially diverse applications. Also, it urged a more thorough study be made of the technology and possible cost savings which might accrue from the diverse uses of lightweight expandable structures in space.

Expandable structure technology for manned space applications was again reported by NASA scientists in 1971 when they revealed the design and fabrication of full-scale airlocks, crew-transfer tunnels, space station modules, lunar shelters and flexible windows.

Also, the NASA results of composite-material fabrication and materials-testing showed promising applications for the space shuttle, space stations, space-based auxiliary structures, as well as for hangars, living quarters, experiment-testing modules, crew-rescue devices and space observation domes. To assure the practicality of constructing three-dimensional space struc-

An eight sided tetherdral radar reflector used as a space refector target. *(Raven Industries)*

Inflated torus and membrane for test in space application. *(L'Garde, Inc.)*

Inflatable antenna concept.   *(L'Garde, Inc. Photo)*

tures, special techniques of fabrication were developed.

NASA scientists at Langley Research Center urged maximum effort be made in employing expandable structures in the manned space program. By 1971, inflatable and expandable structures required no fundamental breakthroughs in technology to become operational. The manifold applications of inflatable, erectable structures provide the least costly opportunity to undertake some valuable missions in space, and

can be seen as a matter of strategic importance to the United States. Political pressures are interwoven with technological progress and success, as shown by the recommendations of a Congressional Committee to the space inflatables already flown in space. Without reservation, the Congressional report encouraged the use of more expandable structures in space and recommended that the Space Agency and the Defense Department coordinate their efforts and consciously set up specific tasks for expandable structures in our national space program.

Toward this goal, a number of designs and shapes have been developed by both private industry and NASA. One design is a large toroid, using inflated spokes, or transfer tunnels to connect the toroid with the central core. While the inflatable space station designs were being laid out with tables, chairs and bunks, details containing permanent personnel, rendezvous technology for crew rotation, and reprovisioning were still being worked out.

Since maintaining an inflatable shape in space by internal pressure could not be counted on indefinitely, particularly with meteoroid occurrences, the space stations ability to hold its shape, or rigidity, was im-

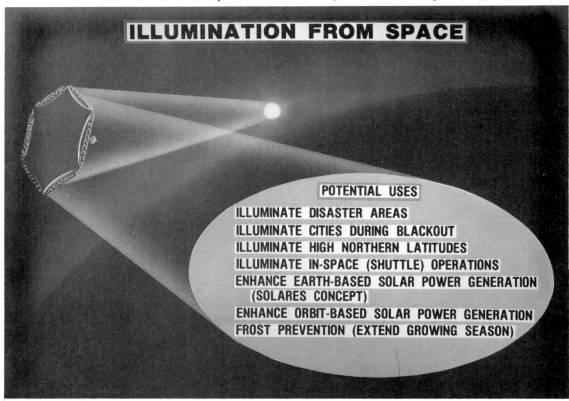

(NASA Photo)

A 24-foot-diameter model of a possible manned inflatable space station for research purposes to obtain basic information on the design and operation of inflatable space stations of the future. The hub at the center could contain an inflation system, life support system, and batteries. The fabric structure is extremely strong and light and is in fact comparable to metal in strength when fully inflated. (NASA Photo)

Inflatable, erectable space station concept. (NASA Photo)

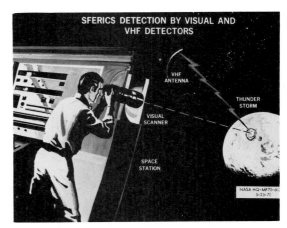

Artist's conception of a centralized and general purpose laboratory in Earth orbit. The space station will use weightlessness, unlimited vacuum, wide scale viewing, and unobstructed celestial viewing to conduct a wide variety of activities. (NASA Photo)

Award winning model of a space station concept by Rene A. Berglund. A space station ready for launching and an inflated model erected in space. (NASA Photo)

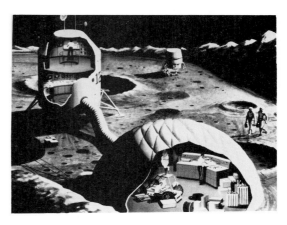

Rendering of possible semi-permanent lunar base including an inflatable laboratory with workshop and control center. A lunar base would represent an opportunity for international, scientific and technological cooperation. (NASA Photo)

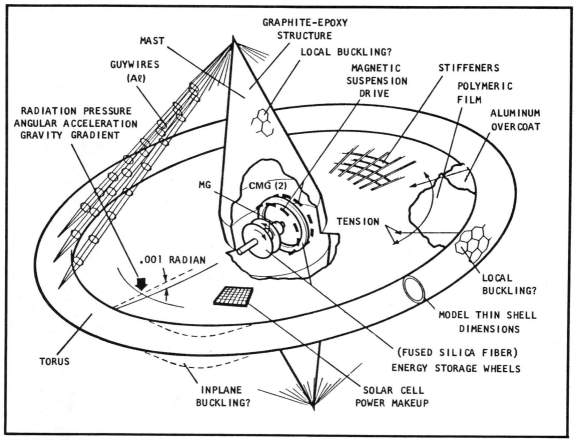

Modular inflatable space station. (NASA Photo)

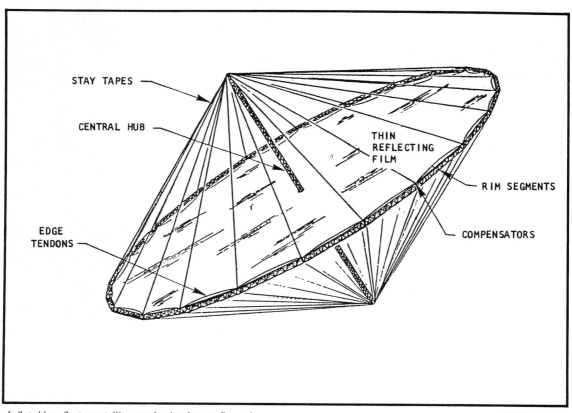

Inflatable reflector satellite-nearly-circular configuration. (NASA Photo)

portant. Anti-meteoroid technology has since provided a number of solutions, including a foaming agent that hardens into a bubble-filled rigid plastic.

One typical application of this technology includes an inflatable solar collector, having a lens and double-wall section filled with foam that becomes rigid when hardened. A wire would then burn away the unwanted half of the balloon structure, exposing the silvered concave surface of the lens to the Sun. Tests have proven this technique to be highly practical. The same approach is suited for directional communications reflectors, and radar and decoy reflectors, each having its own design. Advanced materials used in these expandable space structures are now available.

The NASA scientists confirmed in 1971 the report that the space agency was looking into manned erectable structures, space-applied materials, effects of micro-meteoroids and wobbling, thermal balance, improving the packaging and unfolding of expandable structures, and designing internal arrangements of equipment in complex expandable structures, all a part of the agency's scientific investigations of the universe.

Scientists have long tried to discover how large amounts of sunpower can be used to take care of the electricity needs here on earth. One likely candidate for earth's energy supply is the inflatable solar structure. In 1978 a team of NASA scientists from Ames Research Center recommended the employment of orbiting reflectors, called SOLARES. They examined many alternate sources as substitutes for the cost and limited supply of fossil fuels. The result of their studies identified an environmentally acceptable, renewable resource: solar energy. However, solar-derived electrical energy development in the past had been held back because of the economics of solar farming.

SOLARES, rigid or inflatable, was designed to solve the problem, by providing a continuous and concentrated supply of solar energy to selected terrestrial solar conversion sites. Once in operation, the collective mirror areas could eventually replace the present electrical generating capacity of the world. It was envisioned that the mirrored-structured design would use polymeric film and aluminum evaporated on its face together with a stiffened, open-weave composite structure. The mirrored component would

This inflatable shelter is designed for astronauts' use on the moon. When fully inflated, it accommodates power-generation equipment, temperature control, hydrogen and oxygen tanks, and voice telemetry links. The flexible device could provide shelter on the moon's rugged environment for two weeks. (NASA Photo)

A six-foot metallic balloon called The Integrated Rendezvous Target, was launched in the space shuttle Challenger on February 3, 1984 as part of its payload. It was to visually test and investigate aerodynamics (stability and damping) and identify any atmospheric drag or density.

(NASA Photo)

then be placed on a supporting structure made up of an outer torus, radial spokes and azimuthal stringers. SOLARES could supply electrical energy in excess of that currently provided by the existing system of hydro, nuclear and fossil fuel plants worldwide.

The NASA scientists further believed that the SOLARES system, if financed by the United States, would ultimately allow the U.S. to regain its position of self-sufficiency, and become an energy exporter to the rest of the world, rather than remaining dependent on foreign energy sources. An operating inflatable SOLARES could simultaneously produce electrical power for use by industrial nations while providing the energy needed for the agrarian countries.

Three years before the Ames scientific

report, John E. Canady, Jr., NASA Aerospace Technologist at Langley Research Center, came out with an inflatable reflector structure employing gas to inflate the torus and expand the structure. This SOLARES design would be able to take in large amounts of solar energy which could then be reflected to earth collector sites for conversion to electric power. Canady's design impregnated the skin and other parts of the inflatable torus structure with a gel of polyurethane containing a volatile solvent plasticizer that evaporates soon after the structure is expanded and exposed to the hard vacuum of space. In this way, the structure would no longer be dependent upon pressurized gas to maintain its shape and rigidity.

In 1979 the SOLARES project shifted from NASA's Ames Center to its Langley Center, where the investigation of solar energy, orbiting reflectors and their potential uses continued. A deployable reflector spacecraft has also been under evaluation at Langley. It could be built as lightweight as 10 grams per square meter and a 1-kilometer reflector spacecraft can be packaged into a single space shuttle.

In a report to the Space Science Board on December 28, 1979, Gilbert J. Friese of L'Garde, Inc., presented test data and design features of numerous inflatable structures, which he confirmed had practical applications in space. Furthermore, he emphasized that they were low in cost and weight as well as having low package volume and complexity.

Inflatable, erectable structures can be packaged in small canisters, then shot into space by rocket, and inflated to become massive satellites with as much as 100,000 times their uninflated volumes. The structures are fabricated from plastics and fibers with great tensil strength. They can then be made into a variety of sizes and shapes to perform specific functions such as reflect electronic signals, gather solar energy, provide safe shelter for men in space, become an orbital operating space station or laboratory, provide a space-storage facility for gases and fuels, as well as a platform for astronomical telescopes, etc.

The full exploration of space, which promises to be one of man's greatest adventures, can be realistically achieved with inflatable space structures and aerospace balloon support.

V.

MODERN SPORT

BALLOONING

Sport balloons evolved from the individual experiments and accomplishment of the balloon pioneers. The desire to achieve flight still motivates individuals with a sense of adventure to participate in popular sport balloon activities. Some people, with a more adventurous spirit, use ballooning to satisfy their quest for records to break and "firsts" to accomplish. Ballooning has always attracted its share of drama and adventure. As long as there are people who are daring enough to cast off from the surface of the earth and ascend into the air, the sport of ballooning will remain popular. Experiencing the thrill of flight is what ballooning is all about.

(a) Basic Balloons

The basic balloon design of gas bag, suspended basket, valve and ballast were all developed during the 18th Century. Various modifications have been made since, but in describing a sport balloon, one is still dealing with these essentials. These basic features of the modern balloon were designed in the early 1780's by Professor Jaques Alexandre C. Charles, the French inventor of the valve and the designer of the car suspended from a hoop attached to the balloon. More of Professor Charles' ballooning activities are discussed in Chapter One.

In much the same way, the popular sporting design consists basically of the bag, which is roughly spherical in shape, the gondola and the valve system. The bag is put together in many pieces called gores. Gores are tapered at both ends, and when secured together a sphere is formed. Added to this spherical shape is an extension known as a neck. After inflation the neck is

left open as a safety precaution. A sphere with an appended tangent cone has become the classic balloon design; built to withstand heavy circumferential stresses and have zero stress across the gore seams. This is characterized by a flat top, high equator, and a continuous curvature from the equator to the point of load suspension. Design modifications have overcome the problem of "rotation" by using this elongated form with vertical lobes at the rear. This keeps the nose head-on into the wind and reduces the tendency to drift.

The car, or basket, is suspended beneath the gas bag by a network of ropes passing over it. In early designs, a webbing of thin rope netting was placed over the bag, firmly drawn together beneath the balloon, then tied to the gondola basket. Containers filled with ballast were placed inside and around the outside of the goldola, to assist the balloonist in maintaining the aerostat at a proper altitude as well as its attitude to the wind. Gondolas today are a far cry from the wicker baskets of the past. Modern instruments and controls equip the present-day balloon cars. The instrumentation carried aboard the balloon gondola include an altimeter, a rate-of-climb indicator, a compass, and a pyrometer which indicates temperature inside the balloon. Extending from the basket are the guide ropes which drop to the ground and are used to secure the balloon from rising when it is being inflated with gas.

There have been similar advancements in the valving systems. The valve at the top of the balloon used to release gas from the bag at the proper time, is controlled by the balloon pilot with a line that runs from the

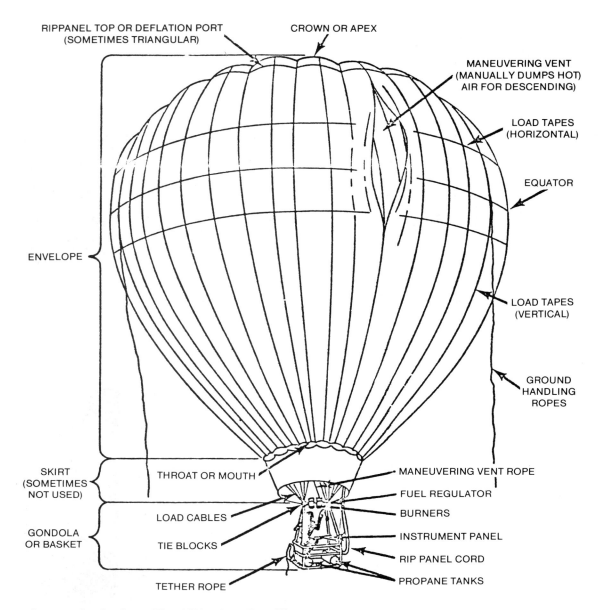

RIPPANEL TOP OR DEFLATION PORT
(SOMETIMES TRIANGULAR)

CROWN OR APEX

MANEUVERING VENT
(MANUALLY DUMPS HOT)
AIR FOR DESCENDING)

LOAD TAPES
(HORIZONTAL)

EQUATOR

ENVELOPE

LOAD TAPES
(VERTICAL)

GROUND
HANDLING
ROPES

SKIRT
(SOMETIMES
NOT USED)

THROAT OR MOUTH

MANEUVERING VENT ROPE

FUEL REGULATOR

BURNERS

GONDOLA
OR BASKET

LOAD CABLES

INSTRUMENT PANEL

TIE BLOCKS

RIP PANEL CORD

PROPANE TANKS

TETHER ROPE

valve to the basket. The "Ripping Panel" device was introduced by American aeronaut John Wise for the purpose of emptying the balloon rapidly on landing, thus reducing the danger of bumping along the ground. More recently, Tracy Barnes, a widely known balloonist, designed a failsafe deflation system that would not collapse the balloon accidently, but could only be opened by the balloonist. The deflation system has a variable controlled vent, using a disc at the apex of the gas balloon envelope.

Balloon material development has undergone similar improvements to those seen in design and assembly techniques; most thanks to the research conducted by NASA, the Department of Defense, the NSBF, the NCAR and the balloon manufacturers.

The ordinary sporting balloon is made of synthetic fabrics like dacron, nylon or plastic material with a special coating added. Its size may range from 50,000 to over 100,000 cubic feet. The materials used in the early fabrication of gas-containing envelopes for balloons were silk or cotton. The Charliere balloon was made of a rubber-varnish-coated silk with a final coat of wax. Since the end of WWII, the polyethylene balloon has come into use. Polyethylene plastic demonstrated its superiority to rubber in high-altitude flights. Also, a polyester called Mylar has been developed, which is about ten times stronger than polyethylene. Mylar absorbs less energy in the solar spectrum and is therefore less sensitive to temperature changes. Sometimes dacron threads are laminated to the Mylar for further strength.

*The flying inflatable chateau—a replica of Malcolm Forbes'
chateau de Balleroy Museum, (background) located twenty
miles from France's Normandy Beach.*
(Forbes Publications)

*Malcolm Forbes, with his son, Robert, completed the first hot-
air balloon record flight across the United States from the
Pacific Coast to the mouth of the Chesapeake Bay, Virginia,
on the Atlantic Coast on November 6, 1973.*
(Forbes Publications Photo)

The first hydrogen balloon was designed by Professor Charles and built by Black in Scotland; Cavello in England; and Volta in Italy. Yet it was the Robert brothers in 1783 who first succeeded in making the envelope impermeable to hydrogen. With today's new fabrics, permeability is less of a problem, but the type of gas used to inflate the balloon depends on a variety of factors. Substances used to inflate a balloon can vary. The basic gases used include hot air, coal gas, helium and hydrogen.

Aside from hot air, hydrogen, helium and coal gas, there have been other possible light gases that could be used for balloon inflation. One is steam .... another is ammonia. In the search for a substitute for the more costly helium, Scotsman W. Newman Alcock revived the idea of the steam balloon in 1950. Steam and air mixture has a much greater specific buoyancy than hot air. The production of steam is merely a matter of the temperature and pressure at which steam is produced. Steam buoyancy is attained at 212°F, with dry steam providing 23 pounds per 1,000 cubic feet. This means that a smaller steam balloon may be used for the same lift as a hot air balloon. The steam balloon is potentially an inexpensive and interesting concept for sport ballooning; however, a workable one has yet to be built. Ammonia also has an acceptable lifting power of 30 pounds

*Malcolm S. Forbes, shown as he piloted his transcontinental
hot-air balloon over eastern Virginia in the final leg of his
world record-breaking flight.*   *(Forbes Publications Photo)*

per 1,000 cubic feet. Its potential advantages are: it's nonflammable, it's storable, it's soluable in water, it's inexpensive and it's available everywhere.

However, the gases generally used in sport balloons are helium, hydrogen, or hot air. Helium is preferred as the lighter gas because it does not burn like hydrogen. Helium lifts 92.64% as much weight as hydrogen and diffuses from the bag more slowly. If contaminated with air, helium can be purified relatively inexpensively, while hydrogen is costly and hazardous.

The crew spreads the balloon out on the ground, then using a "flapping" technique, ambient air is into the balloon mouth.

After the balloon is filled with ambient air, that air is supplanted with hot air from the propane burner.

The pilot directs the flame into the balloon mouth held open by crew members.

The pilot continues to force hot air into the balloon while crew members on the ground resist lift.

As the balloon rises, the basket, which was placed on its side, begins to "translate" into an upright position.

As the balloon lifts off, the pilot and passengers prepare for the coming flight.

Some windy conditions can require the added weight of a crew member while balloon is being heated to liftoff temperature.

The balloon floats gently with the wind, followed by a vehicle on the ground.

(Photos by Brian Lawler, Ballooning Magazine)

The deflation port in this balloon is a circular type.

With a little help from the crew, the balloonist lifts the basket and envelope into a waiting truck.

(Photos by Brian Lawler, Ballooning Magazine)

After landing the balloon, to terminate the flight the pilot pulls a cable which operates a deflation panel in the top of the balloon.

After deflating the balloon, its envelope is stuffed into the basket for storage.

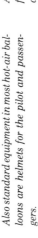

Also standard equipment in most hot-air balloons are helmets for the pilot and passengers.

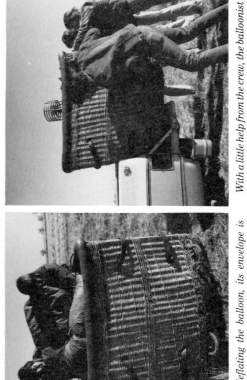

Looking into the deflation panel of this balloon, we can see the inside of the envelope.

Every hot-air balloon carries a dropline that can be thrown over the side for crew members to help restrain during landing.

Once the balloon's deflation port is opened, the balloon starts to sink to the ground.

(b) Balloon Specifications/ Flight System

Sport balloons must be manufactured to meet Federal Aviation Administration regulations, so that the Standard Airworthiness Certificate can be issued on delivery. In FAA certification of a balloon, specifications for the safety of the total balloon system are included. The following is an overview of the features of a sport balloon's flight system and some of the FAA specifications involved.

The Envelope fabric comes in a rainbow of colors and must pass strict quality control tests for strength, porosity and tear resistance. It is treated with special ultraviolet inhibitors to minimize deterioration from the sun and to preserve fabric strength. One manufacturer derives the design of its envelope by computer. It uses the French Fell seam to lock the fabric together and uses tough nylon webbing on the gore seams to distribute the load evenly. Connecting the envelope to the basket is a suspension system of heat resistant steel cable.

The Burner is mounted on top of the rigid gondola uprights, and the rigid superstructure is designed to eliminate the danger of the propane burner collapsing on the aeronaut during landing. A single burner can provide up to 11 million BTU/ hour, with the burner's pilot light virtually eliminating burn-outs. The metering valve can be adjusted to maintain a steady burn; and the gimballed burner mount allows the balloonist to direct the flame for easy inflation.

The Fuel Tank comes with a quantity indicator and meter shut-off valve. An aluminum or stainless steel tank is firmly mounted in the goldola with quick-coupling buckles. A balloon may carry one or two tanks with a capacity of 10 or 20 gallons.

The Skirt completes the envelope design. It protects the burner flame from wind gusts and aids in inflation. The skirt provides an even heat flow distribution for fuel economy and longer flights.

The Deflation System is a pilot-activated rip cord, or strap, which pulls the top cap open for the quick release of hot air upon landing. On some models, a vent system is located high on the side of the envelope for precision maneuvers and for quick release of hot air.

The Gondola (or Basket) contains the fuel tanks, instrument case, passengers of varying numbers, and an optional panel-mounted burner control. The gondola of a sport balloon must be constructed strong enough to carry its static and inertial loads and must accommodate pilot and passengers safely during all aspects of the balloon flight. The flight controls, fuel tank, burner, and other accessories must be logically located in the basket. The flight instruments must be functionally displayed and securely mounted while the navigational charts, tools, igniter and other gear must be securely stored.

The Instrument Components are basically the altimeter, a rate-of-climb meter and a pyrometer, which measures the temperature of internal air at the crown of the envelope.

The Framework must be strong and able to distribute weight evenly. It must also be able to dampen any impact during flight or on landing, in order to help prevent injuries to pilot and passengers.

Ropes between the basket and the load, particularly, must be taut and safely located during flight and drag landings.

Human Engineering of the basket must adequately consider the available and competing space of the pilot and passengers with the fuel tanks, flight instruments, burner, plumbing and other accessories; and each must serve a suitable and integrated functional purpose.

Leading manufacturers of sport and high-altitude scientific balloons include Schjeldahl, Winzen International and Raven Industries. Raven products are diversified ... from sports balloons to space orbital deployment devices. Winzen specializes in large scientific balloons and has the patent on polyethylene StratoFilm which has been used in zero-pressure balloons. Other major balloon manufacturers include Ames, Barnes, Piccard, Cameron, Avian and Hare.

(c) Balloon Operations

The basic operations of the balloon were mastered in the early days and have changed little since. The only specific control is up or down. Vertical flight is controlled by the valve for releasing the gas and by the one that releases ballast, which is usually water or sand. One is never certain about the landing point. Balloon piloting is a skillful operation. A balloon pilot certificate, or license, is issued by the Federal Aviation Administration, and is earned after passing the FAA written examination, logging a specific number of hours in a balloon, a solo flight, a flight to altitude and passing a flight test.

Once the balloon is partially inflated and the basket is attached, the pilot and passengers go aboard the gondola while the ground crew maintain a strong hold on the ropes. The balloon starts to rise as the heavier air outside pushes on the envelope. The pilot, after checking the instruments and the wind, casts off. The ground crew gently releases the guide ropes and some ballast to lighten the load.

Once launched, the balloon rises rapidly and the bag begins to fill out. The heat from the sun's rays expands the gas. When a cloud passes over the balloon, the balloon may descend unless ballast is dropped. As the weight in the balloon and the gas in the bag becomes equal to the air surrounding it, the envelope becomes suspended in the air at the highest altitude level or ceiling. The pilot may seek a certain altitude to utilize winds that will carry the balloon to the

The last race Ward Van Orman made, which ended up in the Canadian wilds. *(Goodyear Photo)*

Gas cylinders used in inflating balloons. *(Goodyear Photo)*

Edwin J. Hill and Arthur Schlosser preparing for a 1931 flight. *(Goodyear Photo)*

Gas inflation for a balloon race, August 1936.
(University of Akron Archives Photo)

destination in his flight plan.

When the balloon pilot is ready to return to earth, he valves down. As the gas is let out, the bag deflates and the balloon descends. The descent is controlled by the pilot, who keeps a sharp eye on the altimeter and wind. On nearing the ground, ballast is thrown overboard to slow down the speed of

descent. By expert piloting, the balloon is brought down to just above the ground and remains almost motionless. Then, with the balloon suspended just above the ground, the rip cord is pulled. The gas bag opens, releasing the gas and the balloon gondola settles gently to the ground, while the deflated bag drops limply around it.

One experience a balloon pilot must be ready for is running into wind shears. The invisible shear boundaries vary in size and velocity. The atmosphere is stratified, with a different wind direction every few hundred feet or so. The top of the balloon is like an airfoil, and normally the balloon drifts at the same speed as the wind, so there is no airflow over the top. But when wind shear is present, air may come faster across the top of the balloon and results in a false lift. This can upset the equilibrium of a balloon and create a potential hazard if it happens close to the ground. Balloonists try to avoid any trouble by simply not flying in heavy weather and not at midday, when the heat stirs up vertical shears that are hard on the balloon. They get up before dawn and fly early in the day when the air is the calmest. Just after sunrise and the few hours before sunset are usually the best times to find ideal ballooning winds.

1912 Balloon Air Races   *(Goodyear Photo)*

(d) Balloon Racing

Balloon racing is a sport involving competition between manned balloons. Pilot excellence is judged by the best conducted flight. Because wind alone determines the velocity and direction of a flight, a balloonist can seldom predict accurately where his craft will land. However, he must know the effects of air currents on height and direction, and how to manipulate valve and ballast for ascent and descent. Competitors participate in a variety of events which include long-distance races, spot landing matches, cross-country activity and hare-and-hounds chases. In a long-distance race, the winning balloon is the one that travels the farthest and remains aloft the longest. In both spot landing and cross-country matches, the pilot must take off and land within a specified time. In the former event, the one who lands closest to the designated spot wins; in the latter, the one who goes the farthest is the winner. In the hare-and-hounds racing, sports cars follow the balloon and the winner is the first driver to reach the landing spot. Balloon racing became an international sport in 1906 with the staging of the first James Gordon Bennett Trophy Race in France. This long-distance event took place nearly every year from 1906 to 1938, and has been revived in recent years.

During the 1950's, despite stringent air traffic controls and the high costs of the sport, enthusiasts from many European

Start of Gordon Bennett Races, Germany, in 1912
(Goodyear Photo)

Start of the National Balloon Race from San Antonio, Texas, April 23, 1924. The race was won by the Goodyear III piloted by W.T. Van Orman and C.K. Wollam.   *(Goodyear Photo)*

Under the "Detroit" balloon at Gordon Bennett races, 1927. *(Goodyear Photo)*

Hydrogen filled balloons waiting for the 1930 Bennett race. *(Goodyear Photo)*

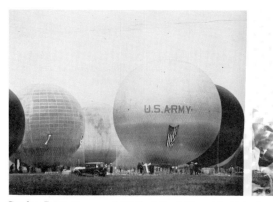

Gordon Bennett races of 1927 at Ford Airport in Detroit. *(Goodyear Photo)*

Gordon Bennett air race, 1930. *(Goodyear Photo)*

countries and the United States brought back free ballooning. Individual crews and clubs from both Europe and the United States gather each year at Murren, Switzerland to make the voyage over the Alps to Italy. This particular sporting event began in 1910 with Edward Schweizer's flight over the Alps. On August 24, 1962, Mrs. Nimi Boesman contributed to the records of this sport with her flight across the Alps, alone in a free balloon. For this outstanding accomplishment, President Lyndon Johnson awarded the Harmon Trophy to Mrs. Boesman on September 16, 1964.

On March 26, 1961, the Balloon Federation of America was formed for the purpose of supervising, sanctioning and documenting official ballooning competitions and record attempts in America. The BFA also promotes, develops, and assists ballooning activities in the United States. The BFA is a division of the National Aeronautics Association in Washington, D.C., which is the U.S. representative to the Federation Aeronautique Internationale (FAI); the recognized world agency responsible for sanctioning, supervising and documenting official aviation competition and world aeronautical record attempts.

One such record was made on April 13, 1963 when the Raven, a hot air balloon, crossed the English Channel by flying from Rye, England to Graveline, France. The flight took just 3 hours 45 minutes, although they carried 240 pounds of fuel, which was enough for 10 hours of flight. The Raven was 50 feet in diameter and held 60,000 cubic feet of air heated to about 180° above the ambient temperature using a liquid propane burner. It was the first successful channel crossing by a hot air balloon and the first attempt since de Rozier's ill-fated flight in 1785 in his combination hydrogen-hot air aerostat.

At a 1978 championship meet at Indianola, Iowa, showing a new Raven balloon just introduced to the public.

(Raven Industries Photo)

A solar hot-air balloon developed by Frederick Eshoo and built by Raven. The near side is transparent and the opposite is black on the interior and silver on the exterior. The balloon is steered electronically by propellers, so that it faces the sun when lift is needed, or partially away from the sun when you want to descend.

(Raven Industries Photo)

Start of International Race at Albuquerque, February 1973.

(University of Akron Archives)

(e) The Flight of the Double Eagle II

One of the most sought-after ballooning accomplishments was that of making a successful trans-Atlantic balloon crossing. Between the 1870's and the 1970's, at least sixteen known attempts were made to fly a balloon across the Atlantic, but all ended up in disappointment or disaster. However, the milestone for sport ballooning was to be established by three men from Albuquerque, New Mexico in 1978.

Ben Abruzzo, the first member of the crew, was a business executive ... a veteran balloonist and an experienced airplane pilot. The second member of the crew was Maxie Anderson, who was also a successful business executive with 29 years of experience as an airplane pilot and balloonist. Larry Newman, the third and youngest member of the crew, was a veteran transport pilot and operator of the world's largest Hang Glider manufacturing plant. The three balloon pilots were supported by a flight team made up of flight director W.C. Wiley; technical director, R. Schwoebel; meteorologist, G. Fischbeck; communicator, S. Parks; and the Weather Service Corporation of Bedford, Massachusetts, which provided the meteorological services.

Abruzzo and Anderson alone had made one previous attempt to cross the Atlantic in 1977, but had failed. They had flown from Marshfield, Massachusetts in their 101,000-cubic-foot Double Eagle I balloon for 64 hours, only to be forced to ditch it in the ocean about fifteen miles short of the coast of Ireland. The balloonists had run into a snowstorm which had blown them off course and cut their radio contact. Fortunately, a NASA satellite had helped track the two-man balloon, and a U.S. Air Force helicopter had been able to rescue the balloonists as the Double Eagle I settled on the ocean. Abruzzo and Anderson learned from that experience, and after adding a third crew member, Larry Newman, they went on to make ballooning history in 1978.

The successful Atlantic crossing was made in the spectacular 160,000-cubic-foot Double Eagle II balloon which was ordered from Yost Manufacturing of Sioux Falls, South Dakota; the same firm that built the first Double Eagle I. The 65-foot diameter, helium-filled nylon balloon was attached to a load ring and then to a catamaran-shaped gondola measuring 15 feet by 6½ feet by 6 feet, which could be used in case of an emergency landing at sea. The catamaran gondola, equipped with a 15-foot mast, was a seaworthy structure mounted on a two-inch tubular steel frame and constructed of plastic foam sandwiched between fiberglass panels. Enclosing the gondola was a tent-like, waterproof fabric. Included in the gondola were communications and emergency equipment, oxygen and a 30-day supply of

The U.S. Congress authorized the President in 1979 to present the Congressional Gold Medal to each of the three Eagle II transatlantic balloonists. Congress has presented gold medals to previous aviation pioneers, including the Wright Brothers, Charles Lindbergh and Amelia Earhart.   *(NASA Photo)*

Double Eagle II — Congressional Medal winner, 1978 Transatlantic Record Flight. Maxie Anderson led a three-man team to complete the first successful Atlantic balloon crossing. (Eagle II Team Photo)

food and water. Also, the gondola carried 5,450 pounds of ballast; 4,850 pounds of sand and 600 pounds of lead. Suspended beneath the gondola was a 35-foot by 7-foot hang glider which was to be flown by Newman when the balloon neared a landing site. The Double Eagle II, including crew, weighed 10,550 pounds and measured 112 feet from top to bottom.

The crew planned to launch the Double Eagle II about sunset to prevent superheating of the helium during the initial hours of flight; then during the evening ascend to the 2,000- to 5,000-foot region. The next day, the crew would take it up to between 7,000 and 10,000 feet and remain at this higher altitude for the rest of the flight. The actual time of flight and landing location would depend upon the wind velocity and direction. The Double Eagle II was expected to float northeast from its launch site toward Newfoundland, and then east or southeast in the direction of the European coast. Winds during the flight were expected to average about 30 miles per hour, carrying the balloon about 700 miles each

day. The maximum distance traveled en route was estimated to be between 3,200 and 3,500 miles. During the flight, NASA's Nimbus-6 satellite was to track the Double Eagle II across the Atlantic.

At 8:41 p.m., in the early evening of August 11, 1978, the three balloonists lifted off from Presque Isle, Maine, in good weather, into a mild current of air. The partly slack, eleven-story, helium-filled envelope looked like a sphere centered on a cone, with their hang glider in tow. The crew climbed to the planned altitude and everything looked good to maintain it. The balloon, however, dropped and stayed at a lower altitude than desired. In order to make sure that Double Eagle II was not leaking any helium, Anderson braced himself as Abruzzo climbed on his shoulders and reached up to open the appendix of the gas envelope and checked inside. But all appeared to be well.

The crew eventually decided to pilot the balloon into a migratory high-pressure system, moving from west to east, which ordinarily occurred in the North Atlantic during the intervals of spring and autumn storms. This high, sandwiched as a ridge between two low-pressure systems, brought the balloon into much higher altitudes and for about one-third of the flight Abruzzo, Anderson and Newman flew above 15,000 feet and were on oxygen. After the fourth sunset, the altitude of the Double Eagle II was 16,500 feet and the balloon began picking up some 300 pounds of ice on the envelope. The crew was unaware of the ice build-up, however, until the next morning when the sun's warmth brought rain showers from the gradually melting ice.

The problem of maintaining equilibrium kept the crew busy throughout the flight. They had to juggle such factors as how much ballast to release at any given time; the effect of the air temperature on the helium gas in the balloon; and weather conditions, which were not entirely predictable, despite reports from their ground support team. Releasing ballast from the balloon could either slow its descent, help maintain an equilibrium, or increase the balloon's altitude. The helium gas in the balloon envelope would contract at night, then expand in the daytime, filling out the envelope and adding to its lifting capacity. Adding further complexities to maintaining this delicate balancing were uncontrollable weather conditions that the Double Eagle II might encounter unexpectedly. For example, about noon on August 16, after a back-to-back experience with ice and storm, the Double Eagle II was riding above 23,000 feet. Blue sky returned briefly, only to be blanketed out by high cirrus clouds. The balloon, cooled by this column of dry, less buoyant air mass, began to descend and, unable to regain equilibrium, dropped down to the 4,000-foot cloud level. The crew carefully released ballast and the balloon once again began to climb ... this time reaching an altitude of 24,950 feet, its highest point during the flight.

In the cooling sunset of August 16, the Double Eagle II gradually floated down to 15,000 feet and the crew sighted the Irish coast. The evening's low temperatures brought the balloon lower than anticipated, so the crew started to jettison some of the lightweight items over the populated area, among them, Larry Newman's hang glider, which he had hoped to fly from the gondola before landing on European soil. The released glider quietly nosed over, executed three loops, then gradually circled slowly downward. Still, during the coolness of night, the balloon dropped to 11,000 feet as the three balloonists looked out over the brilliantly lit Dublin. Not long after, the balloon crossed over St. George's Channel to the Welsh Coast.

As the sun came up over Southern England, the balloon heated up slowly and was at 15,000 feet when word came from their support crew to descend to 10,000 feet in order to maintain a good heading for Paris. This advice was confirmed by wind-aloft information received from a weather station in England. At the higher altitude the winds would have changed the Double Eagle II's course eastward over London with a landing in Belgium; a lower altitude would have caused the balloon to veer south to Brittany.

As the Double Eagle II approached the English Channel near noontime for the long crossing, its oxygen supply had already been exhausted and there was very little ballast remaining. It was with some sense of relief that the Double Eagle II crossed over the mouth of the Seine. As they floated across the city of Le Havre, the balloon and crew were greeted by a jubilant demonstration from the people below.

The French authorities offered to close the Bourget airport at Paris, where Lindbergh had landed, but the balloon team declined the offer, preferring to stay clear of the more populated areas. With the sun setting and time running out to find a place to land, they spotted the town of Evreux from a height of 300 feet. However, they were coming in too low and were forced to heave overboard the empty propane tank and a battery, which dropped harmlessly to the ground. This gave them 2,500 feet to clear Evreux and time to look for a better landing site.

As the Double Eagle II swept over the nearby village of Miserey, their last radio transmission was "All aircraft in the area, Double Eagle II is landing." Dodging buildings, trees and powerlines, the balloon headed toward a barley field about ready for harvest. Ben Abruzzo called out, "Drop the lines!" not wanting the balloon to get too close to the farmer's crop. Maxie Anderson threw some sand overboard, causing the balloon to rise briefly. As it rose, Anderson called out, "Rip!" but Abruzzo had already pulled the main rip panel open, allowing the helium to gush out from the long split in the envelope. The Double Eagle II landed on August 17, 1978 at 7:47 p.m. after having traveled 3,108 miles—a new world's record. The crossing time of 137 hours was also a new record.

Thousands of people from nearby Paris and the other outlying areas had made their way to the landing site. The crew was swarmed with admirers and souvenir hunters who made off with anything they could put their hands on, leaving a tattered Double Eagle II. Abruzzo, Anderson and Newman had rekindled the excitement and spirit of aeronautical adventure, making it clear that, given the freedom and courage, there are no boundaries to individual achievement.

For their act of heroic daring, Abruzzo, Anderson and Newman were awarded the Congressional Gold Medal, recognizing their flight as part of the great tradition of American aviation. The Gold Medal, cast by the U.S. Treasury and carrying a design provided by NASA, was presented at a White House ceremony where members of Congress, foreign dignitaries, government officials and personal friends gathered to honor Ben Abruzzo, Maxie Anderson and Larry Newman. A restored Double Eagle II was placed on permanent display at the National Air and Space Museum in Washington, D.C., as a symbol of the three balloonists who had at last conquered the Atlantic.

(f) Further Adventures

Abruzzo and Anderson were not content to rest with past achievements, however. Less than a year later, in May of 1979, they were off to Long Beach, California, to compete in the prestigious Gordon Bennett International Race with 17 other balloons from around the world.

For this 560-mile overland balloon race, Abruzzo and Anderson flew a smaller Double Eagle III. During the race, temperatures rose in the goldola to 100° and the air outside was unstable. With a 15,000-foot altitude limit placed on the race, they were unable to rise above the turbulent air. Over Nevada, Abruzzo and Anderson were cycling up and down between 4,000 and 5,000 feet. At one point their balloon dropped 12,000 feet to the ground. It bounced back up, but not without their drag lines engaging three powerlines. The drag lines were destroyed, which would make it more difficult for them to land at the end of the race. Then, during the last night, their gondola dragged itself over a mountain just clearing it by two feet. Still, the Double Eagle III completed the race in 47 hours and 7 minutes by landing in a cow pasture three miles northwest of Dover Creek, Colorado, at 9:14 a.m. on May 29, 1979. Upon their arrival back to Albuquerque the next day, Abruzzo and Anderson learned they had won the esteemed Gordon Bennett International Balloon Race. "This race was rough and bumpy," observed Ben Abruzzo, "while crossing the Atlantic ocean was smooth and graceful." However, this new adventure only whet their appetite for new challenges.

(g) The First Transcontinental Crossing

One of these new challenges came in 1980. Balloonists have always considered long-distance, overland flights to be far less likely to succeed than flights over water, because of the unpredictability of thunderstorms which can rocket a balloon up to 100,000 feet or send it crashing to the ground. For this reason, it took many attempts before the first successful nonstop transcontinental balloon crossing of North American was made.

It was Maxie Anderson, veteran of the first trans-Atlantic crossing, and his 23-year-old son, Kris, who finally made the historic coast-to-coast flight. They lifted off on the afternoon of May 8, 1980 from an Army base near San Francisco, in their bluish-gray Kitty Hawk balloon. The Kitty Hawk's gondola, shaped something like a six-pack of aluminum cans, was made of tubular steel covered with fiberglass. The father-son team originally planned to land near Kitty Hawk, North Carolina, to commemorate the Wright Brother's heavier-than-air achievements there at the turn of the century; but the winds refused to cooperate.

Piloted by Maxie Anderson, the 11-story, helium-filled balloon reached speeds of up to 75 miles per hour and was nearly four miles above sea level throughout much of the coast-to-coast flight. Helium balloons are difficult to steer and the Andersons had to maneuver by ballasting and releasing gas to change the craft's altitude and thereby take advantage of the shifting winds. Maxie and Kris had to take turns sleeping four-hour shifts during the flight.

The Andersons outmaneuvered thunderstorms in the Rocky Mountain states by flying over some dangerous weather systems and by outrunning others. The Kitty Hawk headed east and northeast by flying higher than 20,000 feet all the way from Utah to Maine. About 15 hours before they planned to land, the crew and balloon began their descent from the sub-zero temperatures experienced at their cruising altitude.

The Andersons first attempted to land at Loring Air Force Base in the dark, with 23-mile-per-hour surface winds. However, they were advised against it by their meteorological advisor James Mitchell of the Weather Services Corporation, a Massachusetts firm that specialized in balloon weather forecasting. Later, shortly after dawn, the Kitty Hawk hovered over the small town of Grosses Roches along the Saint Lawrence River. When the Andersons cast out the 100-foot drag ropes to slow down the balloon, it became entangled in a 30-foot spruce tree. A helicopter circling nearby was called in to create enough wind for the Kitty Hawk to clear the trees and make its landing. At 7:25 a.m. on May 12, the Kitty Hawk touched down in the meadows of Grosses Roches, Quebec, Canada. The balloon had traveled 2,828 nonstop miles in six minutes less than 100 hours.

Maxie Anderson described the historic cross-country flight as being more difficult than the Double Eagle II trans-Atlantic crossing because of the weather and moun-

One of Goodyear's training balloons.
(University of Akron Archives Photo)

Balloon flight over the Bernese Oberland, the Wetterhorn in background.
(Swiss National Tourist Office, San Francisco Photo)

tains. The father-son balloon team celebrated their new record flight by pouring champagne over each other's head. As to what other challenges may lie ahead, Maxie Anderson suggested a possible balloon trip around the world.

(h) Rosie O'Grady—
World Distance Record

On September 15, 1984, Joseph W. Kittinger set off to be the first balloonist to complete a solo flight across the Atlantic Ocean. Like Lindbergh with the airplane, Kittinger pioneered balloon flight alone across the Atlantic Ocean for the longest solo flight of any type of balloon flown by man. Kittinger lifted off from Caribou, Maine, flying a northeasterly course past Newfoundland to within 300 miles of Iceland, then swung southeast toward France.

As a veteran Vietnam combat pilot, U.S. Air Force Colonel Joe Kittinger flew 483 missions and spent a year as a prisoner-of-war in Hanoi. In July, 1982, retired Col. Kittinger set another world-distance record in the 1,000-cubic-foot, helium-balloon category when he flew from St. Louis to Quebec, a distance of 1,348 miles in 48 hours. As Air Force Captain Kittinger, he set still another earlier world record by jumping from a balloon at 102,000 feet for a free-fall of over 16 miles

before opening his parachute for a safe-landing.

The ten-story, silver and blue helium-filled balloon, named Rosie O'Grady Balloon of Peace, was reaching speeds of 40 to 50 miles per hour at about the 10,000-foot level. Cloud cover didn't allow the sun to expand the helium in the balloon, making it difficult during the trip for Kittinger to fly up to the high-speed winds. Consequently, more ballast was needed to be dumped sooner than planned.

Rosie O'Grady entered the French airspace early in the evening of September 17th in under 68 hours elapsed time after leaving Maine. Instead of landing in the dark, the decision was made to continue flying through bad weather across southern France to Italy in order to break the world distance record. The weather around northern Italy was stormy high winds. Joe Kittinger landed among the trees in the rugged mountains northwest of Savona, Italy, on September 18. The record flight ended some 3,535 miles and 84 hours after liftoff.

The longest non-solo balloon flight reported in the Guiness Book of World Records was 5,208 miles set by the Double Eagle V helium balloon in 1981 in the first crossing of the Pacific Ocean from Nagashima, Japan, to Covello, California. Kittinger hopes that one of his next accomplishments will be a solo record flight across the Pacific Ocean or around the world. Meantime, pioneer and adventurer Joe Kittinger operates the Rosie O'Grady flying circus in Orlando, Florida.

(i) Freedom Flight

Some of the adventures ballooning can lay claim to, however, are not entirely sports or record-winning oriented. Some of ballooning's history involves the dramatic, as well as adventurous. One in particular involved a quest for freedom; not just a freedom of the skies, but a more ultimate, personal freedom as well. The freedom flight of two families in a homemade, hot air balloon from East Germany to West Germany must stand out as one of the most courageous feats of our time. The historic flight was made on September 15, 1979 from their hometown of Poessneck, in a heroic and successful escape to political asylum.

The dramatic escape was inspired by an East German television program on the history of ballooning. Aircraft mechanic Hans Peter Strelczyk, the hopeful pilot, with help from bricklayer Gunter Wetzel, built the hot air balloon based on the principles set forth by the Montgolfier brothers. Strelczyk and Wetzel began by building a cast iron platform with posts at the corners for handholds and rope anchors. Fastened to the center were four propane cylinders which produced the hot air. The balloon which was to carry two couples and their four children, was of homemade construction using curtains, bedsheets, four propane cooking gas cylinders and a metal platform. The 72-foot diameter balloon was stitched together by the wives out of 60 different pieces of materials that the families had bought in small quantities from many shops to avoid suspicion of the authorities.

Two weeks before the successful flight, the two families made their way in the dark of night to a field 25 miles from the East-West border. Their first balloon escape at-

Joe W. Kittinger, Jr., the first to cross the Atlantic in a solo flight by balloon. He holds seven world records, including the highest parachute jump, the longest parachute free fall, and highest altitude reached. (Kittinger Photo)

tempt ended in failure when the gas ran out and the wind direction was wrong. The balloon landed just a few hundred yards short of the West German border.

In spite of their failure, they tried again. This time the balloon lifted off without any difficulty, moving westward at about 15 miles per hour. The two East German families floated apprehensively through the evening sky, over land mines, guard towers, fortifications and self-firing explosives. At one point, an East German spotlight focused on their balloon, but no shots were fired. The balloon had risen to 8,000 feet but started to lose altitude near the border, going down to about 6,000 feet and dropping. When the propane gave out, they were 15 feet above the ground. However, when the balloon finally bumped to a stop in a blackberry bush, the East Germans found they had landed near the Bavarian town of Naila, West Germany. The townspeople of Naila were enthralled, offering employment, money, food, clothing and living quarters to the two freedom-loving families. A very satisfactory end to a dramatic balloon adventure.

Rosie O'Grady Balloon of Peace was specifically built to conquer the Atlantic by designer Paul (Ed) Yost of South Dakota. The balloon's flight system has an 11-story nylon envelope and a fiberglass gondola. The envelope is 83.33 feet in height and 55.55 feet in diameter. The balloon contained 101,000 cubic feet of helium and the envelope's weight alone was 820 pounds.

The upper part of the envelope is made of synthetic fabric lined with an aluminum coating and its lower part is made of black nylon. The color contrast enhances the reflection of the sun's rays during the day and the absorption of the energy lost by the ocean at night. The ballast, mostly sand, helped stabilize the balloon or used to provide lift. Yost also built the Double Eagle II.

A block of four commemorative stamps honoring 200 years of ballooning was issued March 31, 1983, by the United States Postal Service. The left vertical displays the gas balloon Intrepid which was used for aerial surveillance by the Union Army during the Civil War. Thaddeus Lowe made progress reports from the balloon to President Lincoln at 15-minute intervals. The two horizontal stamps in the center of the block form a se-tenant pair. Both stamps depict modern multicolored hot-air balloons in flight. The right vertical stamp depicts the Explorer II, a balloon used jointly by the National Geographic Society and the U.S. Army in 1935 to perform scientific research. The helium-filled balloon, piloted by Captains Albert W. Stevens and Orvil A. Anderson, was used to study cosmic rays, atmospheric conditions and the survivability of living spores at high altitudes.

(Author's Photo)

APPENDIX A
Terms and Tables

Aeronautical Terms

Atmosphere—the air which surrounds the earth.

Aeronautics—the science of traveling in the air.

Aerostatics—the branch of science dealing with mechanical properties of gases in equilibrium, and the equilibrium of bodies held up by them, like balloons and other lighter-than-air (LTA) vehicles.

Aerostation—is the science connected with LTA vehicles not provided with motive power. It is, by use of the balloon, a logical application of the Archimedes' principle.

Aerostat—an aircraft, filled with a gas lighter than air, or hot air, which is supported in flight mainly from the buoyancy derived from the surrounding air. Balloons and airships are aerostats, as well as balloonists, who are also called aeronauts.

Archimedes' Principle—"When a body is completely immersed in a fluid at rest, or in two stationary fluids: one of which lies above the other; the body is buoyed up by a vertical force equal to, in magnitude, the weight of the fluid displaced."

Balloon—a non-powered driven, lighter-than-air craft with a gas bag of impermeable material inflated with a gas lighter than air, or with heated air, and supported by the buoyancy of the atmosphere. The aerostat descends, ascends or floats in air without means of controlling its horizontal direction. The balloon rises if it is surrounded by heavier air and descends when the outside air becomes lighter than the gas within the balloon. The bag, or envelope, of the balloon system must have the capacity to hold enough light weight gas to sustain the load of the gondola, the passengers and equipment in flight at an operational altitude. The development of modern balloons for any atmospheric altitude and for aerospace applications has led to many modifications in balloon design.

Balloons are normally categorized to identify a particular balloon system, including trade names and models. Balloons are also identified by their shape, displacement, type of lift used and the operational use of the balloon.

Most balloons can be scaled up or down in size, built of material of greater or lesser strength or weight and in numerous ways optimized for a specified application. Basic criteria for balloon design include altitude requirements, total payload to be supported and flight loads to be endured.

The original definition of a balloon has now been brought up-to-date to mean . . . any object inflated mainly by gas and no longer restricted to devices hydrostatically lifted within the atmosphere. These can now include devices inflated outside the atmosphere, like erectable space stations, structures and solar-energy concentrators.

This new interpretation for the present-day meaning of balloons has taken into account the historic past and linked them up with the new era of space structures and aerospace balloons.

Some of the original balloon classifications include: **free balloon**—floats in the atmosphere with its equipment, or payload, and is not steered or propelled; **captive balloon**—or tethered balloon, normally held to the ground by a cable; **dirigible balloon**—a powered airship capable of being guided or steered, and capable of carrying passengers and other kinds of payloads; and **unmanned balloon**—without airborne participation of human beings.

Dirigible—a term used as an adjective to first designate a lighter-than-air vehicle inflated with gas lighter than air, and having controlled flight in all three dimensions of space. The term is now solely associated with airships.

Helium—a gas used in lighter-than-air craft. It will lift 92.64% as much load as hydrogen and will not burn as hydrogen does. Helium, the second lightest gas, diffuses from a balloon much slower than hydrogen. If contaminated with air, helium can be purified reasonably and safely, whereas the purification of hydrogen is costly and hazardous.

Aerospace Terms

Aerospace—includes the atmosphere and the regions of space beyond it.

Apogee—is the point farthest from earth in the orbit of an earth satellite.

Artificial Satellite—is a spacecraft or structure that circles the earth or other celestial body. The terms is usually shortened to **satellite,** applying also to natural moons.

Orbit—is the path of a satellite.

Perigee—the point closest to earth in the orbit of an earth satellite.

Period—is the time it takes for a satellite to make one revolution.

Rendezvous—is a space maneuver in which two or more spacecraft meet.

Spacecraft—is a man-made object that travels through space.

Space—begins where the earth's atmosphere is too thin to control objects moving through it. Near the earth's surface, air is plentiful, but higher above the earth, the air becomes thinner and thinner. Little by little, the atmosphere fades to almost nothing, and space begins. Space usually begins about 100 miles above the earth. At this height, a satellite may continue circling the earth for months, or longer, but even there, enough air is still present to slow a satellite and finally cause it to fall. Beyond 100 miles above the earth is not like the air near the earth. It consists of widely scattered atoms and molecules of gas and radiation.

Space Launch—spacecraft or structures are lifted into space atop a launch vehicle. The launch equipment needed to launch a space vehicle depends on the vehicle's size. A small sounding rocket or an inflatable space structure can be launched by a simple launch component. Manned spacecraft is more complex and requires special equipment to be carried to protect the astronauts and bring them safely back to earth. This equipment includes a life-support system, communications and navigation equipment, control system and re-entry and landing equipment.

Inflatable and Erectable Space Satellite—an efficient and economical device that can be packed uninflated in a small canister, shot by rocket into space and then inflated to become a massive space structure, in some cases about 100,000 times its uniflated size or volume. It can be prefabricated into an unlimited variety of shapes and sizes to perform numerous space functions.

Conversion Tables

1 meter.	3,281 feet (39.37 inches)
1 kilometer (1,000 meters).	0.621 miles
0.3048 meter	1 foot
1 cubic foot.	28.316 liters (28.317 cubic decimeters)
1 square foot	0.0929 square meter
1 pound (avoirdupois).	0.45359 kilograms
1 knot	1 nautical mile an hour
1 nautical mile	6,080 feet
1 cubic foot	1728 cubic inches
1 mile	5280 feet (1609.35 meters)

APPENDIX B
Regulations and Safety

Guide to the U.S. government's requirements for balloon pilots, balloon builders, improving safety and preventing accidents.

Federal Aviation Administration (FAA)

In the interest of public and aviation safety, and in the implementation of Congressional legislation, the FAA issued regulations on July 1, 1964, governing the certification of manned-free balloons using gas or hot-air inflation systems. For candidate balloon pilots, the certification requirements were set up as early as November 1, 1962.

Most recent FAA regulations took effect November 1, 1973. Part 61, Federal Aviation Regulations (FAR), prescribes the requirements for issuing private or commercial pilot certificate, with a free-balloon, class rating in the lighter-than-air category. Part 61 contains information relating to pilot operations, procedures and maneuvers relevant to the flight testing needed to be accomplished before issuance of the certificate by the FAA.

Student Pilot Certificate

*must be at least 16 years of age, or at least 14 years of age for a student pilot certificate limited to free-balloon operations.

*must read, speak and understand the English language.

*in lieu of a current third-class medical certificate for free-balloon operations, applicant must personally certify that he has no known medical defects that would make him unable to pilot a free balloon.

Application

*for a student pilot certificate, a FAA form is submitted to a FAA operations inspector or designated pilot examiner, together with the aforementioned medical statement.

Prerequisites for Solo Flight

*must be familiar with the FAA flight rules and have received ground and flight instructions from an authorized instructor or a holder of a commercial pilot certificate with a lighter-than-air category.

*instructions covering flight preparation procedures, including preflight operations; operation of hot-air or gas source, ballast, valves and rip panels; lift-off and climbs; and descents, landings and emergency use of rip panel (may be simulated).

Solo Cross-Country in Free Balloon

*student pilot must receive instruction in the following pilot operation in a free-balloon, solo, cross-country flight: the use of aeronautical charts and the magnetic compass for pilotage; recognize critical weather situations, and the procurement and use of aeronautical weather reports and forecasts; and in cross-country emergency procedures.

Aeronautical Knowledge

*private pilot applicant must complete ground instructions, and be knowledgeable in the following areas: FAA regulations applicable to private, free-balloon pilot privileges, limitations and flight operations; the use of aeronautical charts and magnetic compass for free-balloon navigation; the recognition of weather conditions which could be of concern to the free-balloon pilot; the procurement and use of aeronautical weather reports and forecasts appropriate to free-balloon operations; and the operating principles and procedures for free balloons, including gas and hot-air inflation systems.

Flight Proficiency

*pilot logbook must contain endorsement by an authorized flight instructor in each of the following operations: rigging and mooring; operation of burner, if airborne heater is used; ascent, descent and landing; and emergencies, including use of rip cord (may be simulated).

Lighter-Than-Air Rating—Aeronautical Experience

*an applicant for a private pilot certificate with a lighter-than-air category rating must have the following aeronautical experience: if a gas balloon or a hot-air balloon with an airborne heater is used, a total of 10 hours in free balloons with at least 6 flights under the supervision of a person holding a commercial pilot certificate with a free-balloon rating. These flights must include at least two flights, each one of 1 hour duration, if a gas balloon is used; or of 30 minutes duration, if a hot-air balloon with an airborne heater is used; one ascent under control to 5,000 feet above the point of takeoff, if a gas balloon is used, or 3,000 feet above the point of takeoff, if a hot-air balloon with an airborne heater is used; one solo flight in a free balloon; and if in a hot-air balloon without an airborne heater being used, six flights in a free balloon under the supervision of a commercial balloon pilot, including at least one solo flight.

Limitations of Free-Balloon Rating

*if an applicant for a free-ballooon rating takes his flight test in a hot-air balloon with an airborne heater, his pilot certificate will contain an endorsement restricting the exercise of the privilege of that rating to hot-air balloons with airborne heaters. The restriction may be deleted when the holder of the certificate obtains the pilot experience required for a rating on a gas balloon.

*If the applicant for a free-balloon rating takes his flight test in a hot-air balloon without an airborne heater, his pilot certificate will contain an endorsement restricting the exercise of the privilege of that rating to hot-air balloons without airborne heaters. The restriction may be deleted when the holder of the certificate obtains the pilot experience and passes the test required for a rating on a free balloon with an airborne heater or a gas balloon.

Commercial Balloon Pilot

*to be eligible, must be 18 years of age; able to speak, read and understand English; in lieu of a second-class medical certificate, applicant certifies that he has no known medical deficiencies that would make him unable to pilot a free balloon.

*pass a written, oral and flight tests; and comply with FAA regulations in his rating.

*must have the following flight time as pilot: (if a gas balloon or hot-air balloon with an airborne heater is used) a total of at least 35 hours of flight time as pilot, including 20 hours in free balloon; 10 flights in free balloon, six of these under supervision of commercial, free-balloon pilot; two solo flights, two flights of at least 2 hours duration, if gas balloon is used, or at least one hour duration, if a hot-air balloon with an airborne heater is used; one ascent under control to more than 10,000 feet above the takeoff point, if a gas balloon is used, or 5,000 feet above the takeoff point if a hot-air balloon with an airborne heater is used.

*if a hot-air balloon is used without an airborne heater, ten flights in a free-balloon, including six flights under the supervision of a commercial, free-balloon pilot, plus two solo flights.

The balloon pilot applicant is required to provide an airworthy hot-air or gas balloon for the flight test. The flight examiner tests the applicant on the minimum number of acceptable flight procedures or maneuvers of the free balloon. Emphasis is placed on the safe performance by the applicant balloon pilot. During the entire flight test, an evaluation of the applicant's performance is made, based primarily on his use of good operating practices and sound judgment in avoiding critical situations. Particular importance is placed on necessary precautions taken at launch and recovery sites to avoid endangering spectators or damaging property.

The applicant is further expected to know the meaning and significance of such terms important to a balloon pilot, as, equilibrium, superheat, false heat, never exceed envelope temperature, and the maximum continuous envelope temperature.

The applicant is generally tested on certain procedures or maneuvers within each of the following pilot operations, to determine:

1. **Rigging, Inflating and Mooring**—that the applicant can competently prepare the balloon for flight, determine its airworthiness, and able to follow the recovery procedures after the flight;

2. **Ground and Flight Crew Briefing**—that the applicant knows the essential duties of the ground and flight crews, and that he can competently explain, supervise and coordinate their activities;

3. **Ascent**—that the applicant can accomplish an ascent to a preselected height and be able to maintain that height;

4. **Descent**—the applicant may be asked to demonstrate the proper procedures and techniques for a descent, at an acceptable rate and to a height specified by the examiner;

5. **Landing**—to determine that the applicant can select a suitable landing site and can safely and competently perform various types of landings;

6. **Operation of Airborne Heater** (Hot-Air Balloon)—to determine whether the applicant can start and operate the balloon's airborne

heater in a safe and efficient manner, both on the ground and in flight; and

7. **Emergency Operations**—to determine whether the applicant can react promptly and correctly to emergencies that may occur during flight.

FAA Inspectors Responsibilities

The Federal Aviation Administration (FAA) has provided the following guidelines to its FAA inspectors in applying the Federal Aviation Regulations (FAR) in their inspection of hot-air balloonists.

Regulatory The balloon is subject to the operational requirements of Part 91 of the FAR's, including the minimum safety altitudes of Section 91.79.

Safety The safety rules in balloon operations include: balloon inflation should not be attempted in winds in excess of 10 to 15 knots. This could otherwise result in burning holes in the skirt or throat of the balloon; a launch site should be selected that is compatible with the winds. If there are trees or obstructions downwind, the pilot should assure adequate distance to permit the balloon to climb above them. There should be no attempt to take off close to, or directly upwind of, high tension lines; prior to takeoff, the pilot should assure that his chase crew is thoroughly briefed regarding all aspects of the flight; the pilot should ensure that forecast and existing weather is suitable for the operations anticipated; the pilot should always be alert to the possibility of getting becalmed (unable to drift due to lack of wind) in an unsafe area; If ground speed slows, the pilot should land before drifting into an unsafe area; and, the pilot should never wait until out of propane, before attempting to land.

Business Exhibitions Balloons have been used to publicize business shopping centers, and the like. Under this kind of operation, the balloon is usually tethered and would, therefore, come under the jurisdiction of FAA's Air Traffic Control and Part 101 operation. The operator is encouraged to use a triple or tripod tether arrangement to ensure that the balloon remains clear of all obstructions.

Congested Area Launching When properly planned, a hot-air balloon can be safely launched from a relatively small area, like a football field. Winds are a determining factor. Also, by using tether lines, the balloonist can reach sufficient altitude to clear obstructions, at which time the lines would be released and the climb-out normal.

Public Acceptance Some complaints have been received from ranchers whose animals have become frightened when a balloon passes over. The possibility is that high-frequency emissions from the propane burner created the problem. Balloonists should be cautioned against operating at low altitudes over livestock.

Balloon Races and Meets—Some of the competitive events include:

    a. **Hare and Hound Race**—In the West, this may be called the "Road Runner Race." The lead balloon, the hare, takes off several minutes before the rest of the balloons. The object is to land closest to the target balloon.

    b. **Bomb Drop**—The competitors position their balloons to a prescribed distance from the target. They try then to judge the winds and drop their sack bomb on a target. If the target area is large enough and kept clear, FAA foresees no significant problem.

    c. **Precision Flying**—This event involves climbing to a prescribed altitude at an assigned rate, holding the altitude for a specified time, then changing to another altitude. This resembles a yo-yo event. FAA's interest is to ensure applicable FAA requirements are met and regulations complied with.

FAA's Involvement in Meets FAA has primary responsibility to ensure public safety during the balloon meets or exhibitions. The nature of the site will determine (by the inspector) what safety measures need to be employed. It may be necessary to prescribe limitations as to wind direction and velocity. If the site is situated where calm wind might possibly endanger residents, it may be necessary to prescribe a minimum wind velocity.

Letters of Agreement FAA uses a Letter of Agreement, detailing responsibilities, as a means of control. The sponsor of a balloon meet outlines his responsibilities, including crowd control, notification, communications, etc. In some cases, the sponsor may designate a professional balloonist as the operations or safety officer whose responsibilities are clearly detailed in the letter of agreement. FAA's Air Traffic Control identifies the services provided, like up-to-date weather, a portable tower, or a direct communication line with the tower. The FAA's District Office will determine what aircraft and airmen certification checks may be necessary.

Carriage of Passengers for Hire Persons engage in passenger-carrying for-hire operations, using balloons, are not subject to the requirements of Part 135.1 (b) (7).

Balloon Certification

Part 31, Federal Aviation Regulations, prescribes the following airworthiness requirements for a manned, free balloon, type certificate:

    1. **Flight Requirements**—The balloon must be safely controllable and maneuverable during takeoff, ascent, descent and landing without requiring exceptional piloting skill.

    2. **Strength Requirements**—

        a. **Loads**—Strength requirements are specified in terms of limit loads that are maximum loads to be expected in service.

        b. **Factor of safety**—The 'selected safety factor' is applied to the more critical of the maximum operating pressure or envelope stress; and is applied to the design of all parts of the rigging and related attachments of the envelope to the basket, trapeze or other means provided for occupants. Also to be accounted for are the effects of temperature and other operating characteristics, or both, that may affect the strength of the balloon.

c. **Flight load factor**—In figuring limit load, the limit of the flightload factor must be at least 1.4.

d. **Strength**—The structure must be able to support limit loads without detrimental effect; for the envelope, a test of a representative part is acceptable; and an ultimate free-fall drop test is made of the basket, trapeze or any other place used by the occupant.

3. **Design Construction**

a. The suitability of each balloon design detail, that affects safety of the air vehicle and occupants, should be established by tests and analysis.

b. **Materials**—The suitability strength and durability of all materials must be firmly established by experience and tests; and must conform with approved specifications.

c. **Fabrication Methods**—Methods of fabrication must produce, under close control, and in accord with approved process specification, a consistently sound structure.

d. **Fastening**—Unless free from vibrations, only approved locking devices may be used in the structure (bolts, pins, screws and rivets). Self-locking nuts may not be used on bolts that are subject to rotation in service.

e. **Protection**—Every part of the balloon must be suitably protected against deterioration or loss of strength in service due to weathering, corrosion or other causes.

f. **Inspection Provision**—Each part, requiring repeated inspection and adjustment, must be closely examined.

g. **Fitting Factor**—Any fitting's strength, not proven by limit and ultimate-load tests, would be determined by simulated stress conditions.

h. **Fuel Cells**—Its supportive structures and attachments must withstand, without failure, any inertia loads to which the installation may be subjected, including the drop test. Every part of a pressurized fuel system must be tested to twice the maximum pressure of a normal operation. No part of a system may fail or malfunction during the test.

i. **Heater**—heater used for lift must be designed and installed so as not to create a fire hazard, and that adjacent parts and occupants be protected from heat effects. Heater system (burner unit, controls, fuel lines, fuel cells, regulators, control valves and related elements must pass an endurance test of at least 50 hours. The equipment essential to the safe control and operation of the heater must function under normal and emergency conditions. The test should include three flameouts and restarts, and that each element of the system must be serviceable at the end of the test.

j. **Control Systems**—Each control must perform its functions properly. Captive gas bal-

loon must have an automatic valve or appendix that can release gas automatically at the rate of a minimum of 3 percent of total volume per minute at a maximum balloon operating pressure. A hot-air balloon must have a controllable release of hot air during flight and must have a way to show the maximum-envelope, skin temperature during flight operations which is visible to the pilot.

k. **Ballast**—Each captive-gas balloon must have provisions for the safe storage and controlled release of ballast during flight which are not hazardous to persons on the ground.

l. **Drag Rope**—When a balloon uses a drag rope, the end that goes overboard must be stiffened to prevent entanglement with trees, wires or objects on the ground.

m. **Deflation Means**—There must be a reliable means to permit emergency deflation of the envelope, to allow for a safe emergency landing.

n. **Rip Cord**—The rip cord, used for emergency deflation, must be designed and installed to preclude entanglement.

o. **Trapeze, Basket or Other Means Provided for Occupants**—may not rotate independently of the envelope; and that each object projecting from the trapeze or basket that might cause injury must be padded.

p. **Static Discharge**—Bonding in balloons using inflammable gas is required to insure that any static discharge will not create a hazard.

q. **Safety Belt**—A safety belt, harness or other restraining means, for each occupant, must meet the FAA strength requirements.

r. **Position Lights**—If a position light is required, there should be one steady white position light and one flashing red position light; the lights must be retractable and storable.

4. **Equipment**—Each piece of balloon equipment must be designed and installed to properly perform its intended function with reliability; and to have built-in safeguards against hazards, if it malfunctions.

5. **Other Information**—The manufacturer must furnish a balloon flight manual with each balloon, together with any operating limitations, including the maximum certificated weight. The exterior surface of the balloon envelope must be of contrasting colors, so that it will be conspicuous during flight. Basic equipment required on all balloons include: a compass, an altimeter, and a rate of climb indicator; and for hot-air balloons, a fuel quantity gage and an envelope-temperature indicator.

National Transportation Safety Board (NTSB)
Prevention of fatalities and serious accidents is vital, if sport ballooning is to thrive without intolerable restrictions. Four courses of action by balloonists are recommended by safety expert Dr. Tom Nevison: 1)

seek better knowledge of the hazards, especially inapparent ones, and publicize it; 2) upgrade pilot training at instructor, examination and flight-check levels; 3) recommend change in FAA's regulation, if disparities exist; and 4) assist balloon manufacturers in identifying and correcting any product deficiencies. The National Transportation Safety Board, an independent federal agency responsible for promoting safety and impartially investigating accidents of all modes of transportation, has its headquarters in Washington, D.C.

The aviation accident investigative work of NTSB is two fold: 1) to define the probable cause or causal area of accident; and 2) to apply what it learned to the prevention of accidents. This latter goal is accomplished when the Safety Board, after its investigation, submits its safety advisories directly to the manufacturer, the operator and/or the FAA.

The NSTB investigates all balloon accidents in which there is a fatality while the non-fatal accidents are handled by the FAA. The Safety Board has eleven field offices that are staffed with air safety experts who are especially trained and experienced in aircraft accident investigations. A team of one or more investigators are dispatched to the scene of a fatal accident immediately upon notification of the incident. After the initial onsite examination, other supportive specialists or services may be called to the scene.

NTSB Reported Balloon Accidents—United States (1967–1978)

Year	# of Accidents	# of Fatal Accidents
1967–1975	33	10
1976	13	3
1977	12	1
1978	19	1

Restating the above statistics in another way, NSTB pointed out that between 1973 and 1976, there was a five-fold increase in the rapidly-growing activity of sport ballooning, from 158 to 824 certificated hot-air balloons, in contrast to the annual accident rate between 1974 and 1978, as reported by NTSB, of 11 balloon accidents, 1 fatality and 17 injuries.

Sometimes balloon accident statistics are better portrayed by a brief description of the incident from the following actual NTSB reports, in order to establish the possible cause and preclude recurrences.

1977, near Mosquero, New Mexico, was determined by the NSTB as having an unsafe, gondola design. When the balloon bounced during landing, the gondola turned on its side and was dragged 30 feet by the wind. As the gondola turned over, the pilot's right foot slipped off the gondola deck and was trapped between the edge of the deck and the ground, resulting in a fractured ankle. A similar accident occurred on January 24, 1976, near Death Valley, California, where the balloon encountered high winds and turbulence just before landing. As the pilot executed an emergency rip landing in rough terrain, the gondola turned on its side immediately after hitting the ground. The pilot's legs slipped off the deck and became trapped between the deck and the ground. The high winds dragged the gondola for some 300 yards. The pilot suffered multiple-compound fractures of both legs.

To correct this hazard, the FAA Regional Office contacted the manufacturer about eliminating the dangerous gap in the gondola by lashing a nylon dodger to the deck proper. The NTSB, in its safety recommendation to FAA on this accident, advised it to: 1) issue an Airworthiness Directive requiring the canvas dodger be secured to the deck in order to eliminate the existing gap between the canvas dodger and the deck of the gondola; 2) amend FAA regulation, requiring baskets, gondolas or other enclosures for occupants of manned free balloons be designed to prevent lower extremities from protruding from such enclosures; and 3) for FAA to adopt a rule requiring a manufacturer's maintenance manual on necessary service maintenance and repair information be issued with all manned-free balloons.

One more example of an accident occurred during a balloon festival on October 10, 1979, at Albuquerque, where both occupants were killed. Witnesses reported gusting adverse winds producing side pressure on the envelope of the balloon, which pushed the leading side upward, collapsing the lower half of the envelope. As the rate of descent increased, the pilot fired up both burners to stop the balloon's descent. The flames burned through the fabric and several vertical load tapes. The fabric tore upward, allowing the remaining air inside the envelope to "blowout." The envelope "candled" as the balloon crashed on an asphalt road. The fuel valves and pipe fittings broke off from the butane fuel tanks on impact, allowing the escaping gas to "torch" until the tanks were empty. The NTSB safety investigator retained portions of the unburned envelope fabric for laboratory analysis and his recommended probable conclusion on the accident.

The last incident was where four occupants of a hot-air balloon plummeted to their death on December 15, 1979, at Davie, Florida, after colliding with power lines and being engulfed by flames. One victim attempted a desperate scramble down a rope hanging from the burning red, white and blue balloon but was caught afire by a white flash and flames shooting out. Two of the victims jumped 100 feet to the ground. The balloon, losing the weight of those two individuals, immediately shot skyward, soaring to a height of 400 feet before plunging to the fourth victim's death.

NTSB, in each of the accidents it investigates, makes its final report and recommendation, after determining the probable cause and endeavors to apply what it has learned to the prevention of future accidents.

APPENDIX 'C'
Federation Aeronautique Internationale's
(FAI) Official World Balloon Records* (up to 1980)

CLASS "A"—BALLOONS
Sub-Class A-1
Less than 250 Cubic Meters
7/24/60 **Altitude,** USA, 1,140 meters, 3,740 feet.
Donald L. Piccard, Piccard S-10 "Holiday" balloon, Minneapolis, Minnesota.

8/12/72 **Distance,** USA, 28.33 KMS, 17.60 miles.
Wilma Piccard, Piccard S-10 "Holiday" balloon, Indianola, Iowa.
Duration No official Record Established.

Sub-Class A-2
Between 250 and 400 Cubic Meters
8/24/62 **Altitude,** USA, 5,409.28 meters, 17,747 feet.
Donald L. Piccard, "Sioux City Sue" balloon, Sioux City, Iowa.

5/3/53 **Distance,** France, 208.622 KMS, 129.631 miles.
Audouin Dollfus, "Zodiac" F. AIFA balloon, Senilis to Cheverny, France.

5/3/53 **Duration,** France, 4 hours, 00 minutes.
Audouin Dollfus, "Zodiac" F. AIFA balloon, Senilis to Cheverny, France.

Sub-Class A-3
Between 400 and 600 Cubic Meters
5/10/64 **Altitude,** USA, 11,780 meters, 38,650 feet.
Tracy Barnes, Barnes 14-A balloon, Rosemount, Minnesota.

7/1/22 **Distance,** France, 804.173 KMS, 499.69 miles.
Georges Cormier

3/30/41 **Duration,** USSR, 46 hours, 10 minutes.
Serge Sinoveev, URSS-VR 80 balloon, Dolgoproudnaia, USSR.

*FAI's Official World Balloon Records to 1980.

Sub-Class A-4
Between 600 and 900 Cubic Meters
5/10/64 **Altitude,** USA, 11,780 meters, 38,650 feet.
Tracy Barnes, Barnes 14-A balloon, Rosemount, Minnesota.

4/3/39 **Distance,** USSR, 1,701.81 KMS, 1,056.95 miles.
F. Bourlouski, Moscow to Charaboulski, USSR.

4/3/39 **Duration,** USSR, 61 hours, 30 minutes.
F. Bourlouski, Moscow to Charaboulski, USSR.

Sub-Class A-5
Between 900 and 1,200 Cubic Meters
5/10/64 **Altitude,** USA, 11,780 meters, 38,650 feet.
Tracy Barnes, Barnes 14-A balloon, Rosemount, Minnesota.

4/3/39 **Distance,** USSR, 1,701.81 KMS, 1,056.95 miles.
F. Bourlouski, Moscow to Charaboulski, USSR.

4/3/39 **Duration,** USSR, 61 hours, 30 minutes.
F. Bourlouski, Moscow to Charaboulski, USSR.

Sub-Class A-6
Between 1,200 and 1,600 Cubic Meters
5/10/64, **Altitude,** USA, 11,780 meters, 38,650 feet.
Tracy Barnes, Barnes 14-A balloons, Rosemont, Minnesota.

3/13/41 **Distance,** USSR, 2,766.814 KMS, 1,719.21 miles.
Boris Nevernov, URSS-VR 73 balloon, Dolgoproudnaia to Novosibirski, USSR.

3/13/41 **Duration,** USSR, 69 hours, 20 minutes.
Boris Nevernov, URSS-VR 73 balloon, Dolgoproudnaia to Novosibirski, USSR.

Sub-Class A-7
Between 1,600 and 2,000 Cubic Meters
5/10/64, **Altitude,** USA, 11,780 meters, 38,650 feet.
Tracy Barnes, Barnes 14-A balloon, Rosemount, Minnesota.

3/13–16/41 **Distance,** USSR, 2,766.81 KMS, 1,719.21 miles.
Boris Nevernov, URSS-VR 73 balloon, Dolgoproudnaia to Novosibirsk, USSR.

3/13–16/41 **Duration,** USSR, 69 hours, 20 minutes.
Boris Nevernov, URSS-VR 73 balloon, Dolgoproudnaia to Novosibirsk, USSR.

Sub-Class A-8
Between 2,200 and 3,000 Cubic Meters
5/10/64 **Altitude,** USA, 11,780 meters, 38,650 feet.
Tracy Barnes, Barnes 14-A balloon, Rosemount, Minnesota.

10/5–10/76 **Distance,** USA, 3,983.18 KMS, 2,475.03 miles.
Edward Yost, Silver Fox GB-47, Milbridge Maine to Lat. 37° 11' N. Long. 20° 52' W.

*Credit: National Aeronautics Association, Washington, D.C. (the U.S. member to the international association, FAI).

10/5–10/76 **Duration,** USA, 107 hours, 37 minutes.
Edward Yost, Siver Fox GB-47, Milbridge, Maine to Lat. 37° 11' N. Long. 20° 52' W.

Sub-Class A-9
Between 3,000 and 4,000 Cubic Meters
5/10/64, **Altitude,** USA, 11,780 meters, 38,550 feet.
Tracy Barnes, Barnes 14-A balloon, Rosemount, Minnesota.

10/5–10/76 **Distance,** USA, 3,983.18 KMS, 2,475.03 miles.
Edward Yost, Silver Fox GB-47, Milbridge Maine to Lat. 37° 11' N Long. 20° W. 52'W.

10/5–10/76 **Duration,** USA, 107 hours, 37 minutes.
Edward Yost, Silver Fox GB-47, Milbridge Maine to Lat. 37° 11' N. Long. 20° W. 52' W.
feet.

5/4/61 **Altitude,** USA, 34,688 meters, 113,739.9 feet.
Cdr. Malcolm D. Ross USNR, "Lee Lewis Memorial", Gulf of Mexico.

10/5–10/76, **Distance,** USA, 3,983.18 KMS, 2,475.03 miles.
Edward Yost, Silver Fox GB-47, Milbridge Maine to Lat. 37° 11' N. Long. 20° 52' W.

10/5–1/76, **Duration,** USA, 107 hours, 37 minutes.
Edward Yost, Silver Fox GB-47, Milbridge Maine to Lat. 37° 11' N. Long. 20° 52' W.

Sub-Class AA-11, AA-12, AA-13, AA-14, AA-15
8/12–17/78, **Distance,** USA, 5001.22 KMS, 3,107.61 miles.
Ben L. Abruzzo & Maxie L. Anderson, Co-Commanders, Larry M. Newman, Radio Operator, Double Eagle II, Presque Isle, Maine, USA to Miserey, France.

8/12–17/78, **Duration,** USA, 137 hours, 5 minutes 50 seconds.
Ben L. Abruzzo & Maxie L. Anderson, Co-Commanders, Double Eagle II, Presque Isle, Maine, USA to Miserey, France.

HOT AIR BALLOONS
Sub-Class AX-1
Less Than 250 Cubic Meters
11/2/78, **Altitude,** USA, 3477 meters, 11,407 feet.
Katherine E. Boland, Boland Balloon, Monarch Pass, Colorado.

7/29/78, **Distance,** USA, 4.81 KMS, 2.99 miles.
Katherine E. Boland, Boland Balloon, Farmington, Connecticut.

7/29/78, **Duration,** USA, 30 minutes, 5 seconds.
Katherine E. Boland, Boland Balloon, Farmington, Connecticut.

Sub-Class AX-2
Between 250 and 400 Cubic Meters
11/2/78, **Altitude,** USA, 3477 meters, 11,407 feet.
Katherine E. Boland, Boland Balloon, Monarch Pass, Colorado.

3/13/75, **Distance,** USA, 18.01 KMS, 11.19 miles.
Donna Wiederkehr, Modified Raven Hot Air Balloon, St. Paul, Minnesota.

3/13/75, **Duration,** USA, 2 hours, 40 minutes.
Donna Wiederkehr, Modified Raven Hot Air Balloon, St. Paul, Minnesota.

Sub-Class AX-3
Between 400 and 600 Cubic Meters
11/1/78, **Altitude,** USA, 4642 meters, 15,231 feet.
Brian Boland, Boland Balloon, Fairplay, Colorado.

8/27/78, **Distance,** USA, 57.30 KMS, 35.60 miles.
Brian Boland, Boland Balloon, Bridgeport, Connecticut/Long Island Sound, New York.

8/27/78, **Duration,** USA, 3 hours, 46 minutes.
Brian Boland, Boland Balloon, Bridgeport, Connecticut/Long Island Sound, New York.

10/12/78, **Altitude,** Hong Kong, 6,941 meters, 22,766.48 feet.
Capt. Geoff Green, Cameron C-031, Northan, W.A. Australia.

3/19/73, **Distance,** USA, 137.48 KMS, 85.43 miles.
Matt H. Wiederkehr, Raven S40 Balloon, St. Paul, Minnesota.

3/19/73, **Duration,** USA, 5 hrs. 5 mins. 55 secs.
Matt H. Wiederkehr, Raven S40 Balloon, St. Paul, Minnesota.

Sub-Class AX-5
Between 900 and 1,200 Cubic Meters
2/19/79, **Altitude,** USA, 7546.84 meters, 24,760 feet.
Carol Davis, Firefly, Moriarty, New Mexico.

11/18/78, **Distance,** UK, 178 KMS, 110.6 miles.
Simon Faithfull, Balloon Thunder, Munster-Eversen FRG.

3/19/73, **Duration,** USA, 5 hrs. 5 mins. 55 secs.
Matt H. Wiederkehr, Raven S40 Balloon, St. Paul, Minnesota.

Sub-Class AX-6
Between 1,200 and 1,600 Cubic Meters
8/26/77, **Altitude,** UK, 9,296.4 meters, 30,492.19 feet.
G. Green, Cameron O-56, Northam, Australia.

3/23/74, **Distance,** USA, 369.99 KMS, 288.04 miles.
Denise Wiederkehr, Raven S55A Balloon, St. Paul, Minn. to Waupun, Wisconsin.

4/17/78, **Duration,** UK, 11 hours, 20 minutes.
Julian R. P. Nott, Thunder 56 A, Pitch Green–Barrow Hann, New Holland.

Sub-Class AX-7
Between 1,600 and 2,200 Cubic Meters
6/10/76, **Altitude,** UK, 11,286 meters, 37,027.5 feet.
Julian R. P. Nott, Thunder, Kurman, Republic of South Africa.

1/25/78, **Distance,** UK, 564.47 KMS, 350.74 miles.
Philip Clark, Cameron "Sungas", Bristol, U.K.

3/7/74, **Duration,** USA, 16 hours, 16 minutes.
Matt H. Wiederkehr, Raven S55A Balloon, St. Paul, Minn., to Butte, Nebraska.

Sub-Class AX-8
Between 2,200 and 3,000 Cubic Meters
9/27/75, **Altitude,** USA, 11,822.91 meters, 38,789 feet.
Kingswood Sprott, Jr., Raven S60A Balloon, Lakeland, Florida.

1/25/78, **Distance,** UK, 564.47 KMS, 350.74 miles.
Philip Clark, Cameron "Sungas", Bristol, U.K.

3/7/74, **Duration,** USA, 16 hours, 16 minutes.
Matt H. Wiederkehr, Raven S55A Balloon, St. Paul, MN to Butte, NE.

Sub-Class AX-9
Between 3,000 and 4,000 Cubic Meters
8/1/79, **Altitude,** USA, 16,154.4 meters, 53,000 feet.
Chauncey M. Dunn, Raven S-66-A Balloon N-5682-C, Indianola, Iowa.

1/25/78, **Distance,** UK, 564.47 KMS, 350.74 mi.
Philip Clark, Cameron "Sungas", Bristol, UK

3/7/74, **Duration,** USA, 16 hours, 16 minutes.
Matt H. Wiederkehr, Raven S55A Balloon, St. Paul, MN to Butte, NE.

Sub-Class AX-10, AX-11, AX-12, AX-13, AX-14, AX-15
Over 4,000 Cubic Meters
8/1/79, **Altitude,** USA, 16,154.4 meters, 53,000 feet.
Chauncey M. Dunn, Raven S-66-A Balloon N-5682-C, Indianola, IA.

1/25/78, **Distance,** UK, 564.47 KMS, 350.74 mi.
Philip Clark, Cameron "Sungas", Bristol, UK

11/21/75, **Duration,** UK, 18 hours, 56 minutes.
Donald A. Cameron, Cameron A-500

CLASS "AM"—BALLOONS
Sub-Class AM-10
Between 4,000 and 6,000 Cubic Meters
7/26–30/78 **Distance,** UK, 3,339.086 KMS, 2,074,81 miles.
Donald Cameron, Christopher Davey, Balloon Cameron, St. Johns, Newfoundland, Bay of Biscay.

7/26–30/78 **Duration,** UK, 96 hours, 24 minutes.
Donald Cameron, Christopher Davey, Balloon Cameron, St. Johns, Newfoundland, Bay of Biscay.

Sub-Class AM-11
Between 6,000 and 9,000 Cubic Meters
7/26–30/78 **Distance,** UK, 3,339.086 KMS, 2,074.81 miles.
Donald Cameron, Christopher Davey, Balloon Cameron, St. Johns, Newfoundland, Bay of Biscay.

7/26–30/78 **Duration,** UK, 96 hours, 24 minutes.
Donald Cameron, Christopher Davey, Balloon Cameron, St. Johns, Newfoundland, Bay of Biscay.

Sub-Class AM-12
Between 9,000 and 12,000 Cubic Meters
7/26–30/78 **Distance,** UK, 3,339.086 KMS, 2.074.81 miles.
Donald Cameron, Christopher Davey, Balloon Cameron, St. Johns, Newfoundland, Bay of Biscay.

7/26–30/78 **Duration,** UK, 96 hours, 24 minutes.
Donald Cameron, Christopher Davey, Balloon Cameron, St. Johns, Newfoundland, Bay of Biscay.

Sub-Class AM-13
Between 12,000 and 16,000 Cubic Meters
7/26–30/78 **Distance,** UK 3,339.086 KMS, 2,074.81 miles.
Donald Cameron, Christopher Davey, Balloon Cameron, St. Johns, Newfoundland, Bay of Biscay.

7/26–30/78 **Duration,** UK, 96 hours, 24 minutes.
Donald Cameron, Christopher Davey, Balloon Cameron, St. Johns, Newfoundland, Bay of Biscay.

Sub-Class AM-14
Between 16,000 and 22,000 Cubic Meters
7/26–30/78 **Distance,** UK 3,339.086 KMS, 2,074.81 miles.
Donald Cameron, Christopher Davey, Balloon Cameron, St. Johns, Newfoundland, Bay of Biscay.

7/26–30/78 **Duration,** UK, 96 hours, 24 minutes.
Donald Cameron, Christopher Davey, Balloon Cameron, St. Johns, Newfoundland, Bay of Biscay.

Sub-Class AM-15
Between 22,000 Cubic Meters and above
7/26–30/78 **Distance,** UK 3,339.086 KMS, 2,074.81 miles.
Donald Cameron, Christopher Davey, Balloon Cameron, St. Johns, Newfoundland, Bay of Biscay.

7/26–30/78 **Duration,** UK, 96 hours, 24 minutes.
Donald Cameron, Christopher Davey, Balloon Cameron, St. Johns, Newfoundland, Bay of Biscay.

INDEX (Subject)